Quantification Addendum: International Medical Guide for Ships, Third Edition

World Health Organization

WHO Library Cataloguing-in-Publication Data

Quantification addendum: international medical guide for ships, third edition

1. Naval medicine. 2. Ships. 3. Sanitation. I. World Health Organization.

ISBN 978 92 4 154799 4 (NLM classification: WT 500)

CONTENTS

1. Background

The third edition of the *International Medical Guide for Ships* was published by the World Health Organization, in collaboration with the International Labour Organization and the International Maritime Organization in 2007. The Guide provides advice to help promote and protect the health of seafarers. An important section in the Guide is the 'Ship's Medicine Chest'. This section provides a recommended list of medicines that ships at sea should carry, as well as indications and dosing. The second edition of the Guide, published in 1988, also provided suggested quantities of medicines that ships of various size should hold; recommended quantities were not included in the third edition. The University of Newcastle WHO Collaborating Centre for Training in Pharmaco-economics and Rational Pharmacotherapy was commissioned to develop a list of recommended quantities of medicines listed in the third edition of the *International Medical Guide for Ships*.

2. Scope of project

1. To update the list of recommended medicines in the 'The ship's medicine chest' section of the *International Medical Guide for Ships* to include recommended quantities of medicines required to be held by ships;
2. To develop a list of recommended stock holdings for the medicines listed in the *International Medical Guide for Ships*. The listing will be standardized to quantities per number of crew.

3. Methods

This text was developed in three steps:

1. Mapping the currently recommended medicines to the list of medicines (with quantities) listed in the previous edition of the *International Medical Guide for Ships*.
2. Reviewing the published literature on medicine utilisation and medical requests made by ships.
3. Contacting local maritime services for guidance on supply and medicine use aboard ships.

3.1 Mapping the current medicines list to the quantities in the previous edition of the *International Medical Guide for Ships*

The second edition of the International Medical Guide for Ships provided recommended quantities for 83 medicines. The recommendations were based on three types of ships:

- Ocean-going ships with crews of 25–40 and no doctor (Category A);
- Coastal ships with crews of up to 25 that travel no more than 24 hours from a port of call (Category B); and
- Small boats and private craft with crews of 15 or fewer, and usually travelling no more than a few hours from a port of call (Category C).

The stock levels for Category A and B ships were based on six months' supply. Medicines listed in the third edition of the Guide were compared to those listed in the second edition to obtain an initial estimate of quantities required. This estimate was then modified by taking into account the results of a literature search, discussions with local maritime authorities and storage requirements and expiry of stock. Estimates for the quantity of medicines newly listed in the third edition of the Guide were based on literature review and interviews with local maritime staff.

3.2 Literature review and review of maritime websites

A literature review was done to identify any published data on medicine utilization on ships, and the types of medical conditions that are treated on ships. The search involved major biomedical databases including *Embase* and *Medline*, using terms including 'ship$', 'maritime', seafarer', 'sailor', 'naval medicine', with 'drug use', 'drug utilisation', 'medic$ or drug and suppl$ or procur', 'emergenc$'. Hand searching of key journals, such as International Maritime Health, was undertaken. National maritime websites, such as the Australian Maritime Safety Authority (http://www.amsa.gov.au/), and the Maritime and Coast Guard Agency (http://www.mcga.gov.uk/) were also searched. The information found was used to locate references to the types of medical care required at sea and to refine the recommended stock levels of medicines to be kept.

3.3 Interviews with local maritime authorities and medicine suppliers

Newcastle is one of the largest ports in Australia and as such has a significant maritime industry. Contact was made with local maritime authorities to discuss and refine the recommended medicine holdings. Suppliers of medicines to ships were also identified.

4. Results

4.1 Mapping the current medicines list to the quantities in the second edition of the Guide

Details of the mapping can be found in Annex 1. Fifty (50) medicines are listed in the third edition of the Guide, compared to 83 in the second edition. Only 17 of the medicines (34%) in the third edition were listed in the second edition. There were a further 16 medicines (32%) in the third edition which were similar to medicines in the second edition. However, in many instances the drugs used in the second edition had a different range of indications making a direct comparison difficult (e.g. erythromycin in the second edition compared to azithromycin in the third edition), or had multiple indications in the second edition (e.g. chloroquine for the treatment and prophylaxis of malaria in the second edition, whereas there is no prophylactic medication for malaria in the third edition, only treatment).

Of the 50 medicines in the third edition, only 8 (16%) were recommended to be held by Category C ships in the second edition, with a further 5 (10%) having a similar medicine recommended in the second edition of the Guide.

4.2 Literature review and review of maritime websites

Literature review

Medline and Embase searches identified 106 and 22 potentially useful articles respectively. Based on a review of the titles and abstracts only four articles were identified for review. Articles were excluded if they were non-English, only discussed warships, or if they only discussed passenger ships/ferries.

McKay reported a retrospective analysis of cases where shipboard carers contacted Maritime Medical Access, a company that uses satellite technology to link ships with an emergency physician.[1] The paper reported on 866 cases over 48 months. The most common conditions requiring assistance were respiratory infections such as colds and bronchitis (15%), abdominal complaints such as nausea and vomiting (10%), genitourinary complaints such as dysuria and testicular pain, non-traumatic skin lesions such as rashes (8%), and general dental conditions such as toothache (7%). The most common medications used were analgesics and antibiotics.

Hall et al. reported on the establishment of the Medical Telecommunications Response Center (MTRC).[2] The Center is based near Washington DC in the United States of America and is designed to focus on maritime health issues. Ships contact the centre via satellite where they can then get advice from a physician. A review of 150 consecutive cases reported to the Center identified traumatic injuries (e.g. lacerations) and gastrointestinal disorders (e.g. gastroenteritis) as the most common disorders. Others included musculoskeletal disorders (e.g. muscle strain), ear, nose and throat disorders (e.g. otitis media), and respiratory disorders (e.g. pneumonia and bronchitis).

Scott et al. reviewed the medical problems seen at sea,[3] reporting a retrospective review of 700 medical cases managed by Maritime Medical Access at the George Washington University. The most common problems encountered were acute injuries, followed by infectious diseases (e.g. upper respiratory tract infections). Other complaints included gastrointestinal (e.g. vomiting, diarrhoea and gastroenteritis), cardiovascular (e.g. chest pain), and dermatological problems. Among the most commonly used medicines were analgesics (e.g. paracetamol), non-steroidal anti-inflammatory drugs and muscle relaxants.

Lateef and Anantharaman reported on 21 years' experience of providing medical advice to ships from the Singapore General Hospital.[4] There were over 2,300 calls received, with abdominal pain (25%), musculoskeletal pain and minor trauma (13%), fever with upper respiratory tract infections (12%), renal colic (6%) and chest pain (5%) being the most common complaints. The most commonly prescribed medicines were analgesics, muscle relaxants, antibiotics (e.g. amoxicillin, metronidazole, erythromycin), antihistamines, sedatives, anti-anginals and antacids.

A limitation of all of these published reviews is that they may represent more severe presentations, as they are all based on calls to medical centres; in the third edition of the Guide, 37 (72%) of the medications listed can be used without the need to contact a doctor. Further, none of the reviews gave a clear indication of the amounts of medicines consumed on ships.

Hand searching of *International Maritime Health* located no additional useful information.

Review of maritime websites

The review of international maritime websites identified guidelines in Australia, the United Kingdom (UK) and the United States of America (USA) related to the medicines that should be carried by ships.[5–7]. The guidelines from the USA only listed medicines that a ship should carry and did not provide any recommended quantities. Therefore, these guidelines were not used. The Australian guidelines provided recommended quantities for pharmaceuticals for three categories of ships. Category A ships are seagoing vessels on unlimited voyages during which stores can be restocked from ports and the quantities suggested are based on a crew size of approximately 20. Category B vessels are seagoing ships on short voyages, generally not exceeding 240 kilometres from the nearest port. Category C ships are those that sail in smooth or partially smooth waters and stay close to shore; the assumed crew sizes are not given for Category B and C ships in the Australian guidelines. The UK guidelines also provide advice on three categories of ships; the descriptions of the categories in the UK guidelines are similar to those in the Australian guidelines. In the UK guidelines the quantities are given for each 10 members of crew. The quantities recommended in both of these guidelines were mapped to the medicines in the third edition of the Guide (Annex 2).

Of the 50 medicines listed in the third edition of the Guide, 25 (50%) are recommended in the Australian and UK guidelines for Category A and B ships. For a further 11 (22%) drugs in the third edition there are comparable medicines in the Australian and/or UK guidelines. Only 4 of the medicines (8%) in the third edition of the Guide were listed in the Australian and/or UK guidelines for Category C ships.

Other relevant literature

The International Pharmaceutical Federation (Federation Internationale Pharmaceutique, FIP) has issued guidance on provisioning ships with medicines.[8] This document makes the following points which are relevant to changes since the second edition of the Guide:

- due to the decrease of crew numbers on most ships, the quantities of individual medicines held in stock should be reduced;
- obsolete medicines should be replaced by up-to-date products, selected in accordance with current evidence-based, rational pharmacotherapy;
- the list of products to be held in stock should be updated more frequently;
- a standardised labelling system and appropriate information on use, applicable in all countries in the world, should be introduced.

The International Maritime Health Association (IMHA) has issued a joint statement with the WHO Collaborating Centre for the Health of Seafarers on the quantities that should be held by ships.[9] The guidance is for ocean-going merchant vessels for a 3-week trip. This is similar to the description of Category A vessels in the Australian and UK guidelines, although the duration of the travel is not stated in the Australian and UK guidelines. These quantities are available from the IMHA website and the 3-week ocean-going categorization has been included in Section 5.2 below.

4.3 Interviews with local maritime authorities and medicine suppliers

Captain Guy Plumridge provided information based on his current practice and two decades of experience in the shipping industry, as pertains to the ordering, administration and documentation of medicines on Category A and B ships. Two local suppliers of medicine were identified: Jon Dickson Pharmacy (Mayfield, New South Wales) and St John's Ambulance Australia (Sydney, New South Wales) and interviewed.

5. Proposed quantities of medicines for the third edition of the Guide

5.1 Assumptions and definitions

Categories of ships

The categories used in previous guidelines are summarised in Table 5.1.

The definitions are similar across the guidelines. Therefore, we have used the definitions in the second edition of the Guide when recommending quantities for the third edition.

Table 5.1 Definition of categories of ships used in existing guidelines

	Category A	**Category B**	**Category C**
Second edition of the Guide	Ocean-going merchant vessels without a doctor on board.	Merchant vessels engaged in coastal trade or going to nearby ports, and not more than 24 hours away from a port of call.	Fishing boats or private craft that are never more than a few days from home port, or only a few hours from a port of call.
Australian guidelines	Seagoing vessel on unlimited voyages, and assumes that supplies can be re-stocked if necessary from wayports.	Seagoing vessel on short voyages, generally not extending more than 150 miles [approximately 240 km] from the nearest port. Can be extended up to 200 miles [approximately 320 km] if continuously within range of a helicopter rescue service.	Ships in smooth or partially smooth water, and those that stay close to shore.
UK guidelines	Seagoing or sea-fishing vessels with no limitation on length of trips.	Seagoing or sea-fishing vessels making trips of less than 150 nautical miles [approximately 280 km] from the nearest port with adequate medical equipment. This category is extended to seagoing or sea-fishing vessels which make trips of less than 175 nautical miles [approximately 325 km] from the nearest port that has adequate medical equipment and which remain continuously within range of helicopter rescue services.	Harbour vessels, boats and craft staying very close to shore (generally no more than 60 nautical miles [approximately 110 km] out from shore) or with no cabin accommodation other than a wheelhouse.
IMHA recommendations	Ocean-going merchant vessels without a doctor on board	Merchant vessels without a doctor that are engaged in coastal trade and not more than 24 hours from a port of call.	Fishing or private vessels

Table 5.2 Definition of crew sizes of ships used in existing guidelines

	Category A	Category B	Category C
Second edition of the Guide	Six months' inventory for a crew of 25-40 persons	Six months' inventory for a crew of approximately 25	Crew of approximately 15
Australian guidelines	Crew of about 20 people	Not stated	Not stated
UK guidelines	Per 10 crew	Per 10 crew	Per 10 crew
IMHA recommendations	Per 10, 20, 30 and 40 crew for 3 weeks	Not given	Not given

Crew sizes and trip durations

The crew sizes and trip durations used in previous guidelines are summarised in Table 5.2.

In calculating the quantities for the third edition of the Guide we have chosen to calculate quantities per 10 crew, similar to the UK guidelines. We have normalised the recommended quantities in the second edition of the Guide and the Australian guidelines to 'per 10 crew'. We assumed a crew of 30 and 40 for Category A (a range is given in the details provided below), and 20 for Category B and C ships for the second edition of the Guide, and a crew of 20 for Category A, B and C for the Australian guidelines. IMHA only provided guidance on Category A vessels.

Trip durations are not stated in the Australian and UK guidelines. We have used the IMHA estimate of 3 to 4 weeks.

Pack sizes and shelf life

Given that ships obtain medicines from different countries, it is not possible to recommend exact pack sizes. In most instances, the closest pack size should be stocked. In some cases – topical preparations such as creams, eye drops, or ear preparations – the number of people likely to require treatment has been estimated and a whole tube/bottle/pack per patient is recommended. These recommendations are noted in the comments section of the draft list (Annex 3).

The shelf lives of products have been sourced, unless otherwise indicated, from summaries of product characteristics (http://emc.medicines.org.uk/). The shelf life has been taken into account when making recommendations on the quantities for the third edition of the Guide. However, it should be noted that most medicines have shelf lives of over 24 months and therefore shelf life had little impact on the recommendations.

5.2 Details of the proposed quantities

Acetylsalicylic acid 300mg tablets

Indication(s): Pain, fever and inflammation; prevention of blood clots in angina and myocardial infarction

Dose(s): Pain/fever/inflammation: 600mg–1000mg four times a day

Prevention of blood clots: 100mg–150mg daily

Existing recommendations:

second edition: Six hundred (600) tablets for Category A ships and 300 for Category B ships (equivalent to 150–200 tablets per 10 crew for Category A, and 75–100 per 10 crew for Category B). Category C ships were required to carry 200 tablets. No other nonsteroidal anti-inflammatory drugs were recommended in the second edition.

Australian guidelines: Not listed. Other nonsteroidal anti-inflammatory drugs recommended include diclofenac, ibuprofen, mefenamic acid and naproxen.

UK guidelines: Not listed. Other nonsteroidal anti-inflammatory drugs recommended include ibuprofen and diclofenac.

IMHA guidance: Category A ships should carry 100 acetylsalicylic acid 300mg tablets per 10 crew.

Note: The third edition of the Guide also includes ibuprofen and this is a safer anti-inflammatory agent. Further, it also includes paracetamol as an alternative analgesic and antipyretic. Therefore, acetylsalicylic acid should be reserved primarily for use as an anti-thrombotic and used as a second-line anti-inflammatory/analgesic/antipyretic.

Shelf life: 36 months

Recommendations:	Category A:	50 tablets per 10 crew
	Category B:	50 tablets per 10 crew
	Category C:	Nil

Aciclovir 400mg tablets

Indication(s): primary or recurrent herpes simplex infection; severe varicella (chicken-pox) and herpes zoster (shingles) infection

Dose(s): Herpes zoster: 800mg five times a day for seven days

Other herpes: 400mg five times a day for five to ten days (for three to five days for recurrence)

Existing recommendations:

The second edition of the Guide, and the Australian and UK guidelines did not provide quantities for aciclovir tablets. No equivalent product is listed in these guides.

IMHA guidance: Category A should carry 35 aciclovir 400mg tablets for 10–20 crew, and 70 for 30–40 crew.

Note: Based on the indication in the third edition of the Guide that requires the maximum number of tablets, a single course requires 70 tablets.

Shelf life: 48 months

Recommendations:	Category A:	70 tablets irrespective of crew size
	Category B:	35 tablets irrespective of crew size
	Category C:	Nil

Adrenaline injection 1mg/ml

Indication(s): Anaphylaxis and severe asthma

Dose(s): 0.5ml, the dose may be repeated several times every 5 minutes until blood pressure, pulse and breathing improve

Existing recommendations:

Second edition: Twenty (20) ampoules for Category A and 10 ampoules for Category B ships (equivalent to 5 to 10 ampoules per 10 crew for Category A, and 2.5 ampoules per 10 crew for Category B ships). Category C ships were required to carry 10 ampoules.

Australian guidelines: Category A and Category B ships should carry 5 ampoules irrespective of crew size.

UK guidelines: Category A ships should carry 10 ampoules irrespective of crew size and/or 5 Epipen® per 10 crew, and Category B ships should carry 5 ampoules irrespective of crew size and/or 5 Epipen® per 10 crew.

IMHA guidance: Category A ships should carry 10 ampoules irrespective of crew size.

Shelf life: 24 months

Recommendations:	Category A:	10 ampoules irrespective of crew size
	Category B:	5 ampoules irrespective of crew size
	Category C:	5 ampoules irrespective of crew size

Tetracaine (amethocaine) eye drops 0.5% 1ml individual vials

Indication(s): local anaesthesia for eye examinations and procedures

Dose(s): two drops

Existing recommendations:

Second edition: Two (2) bottles (10ml each) of tetracaine (amethocaine) eye drops for Category A ships, and one bottle for Category B.

Australian guidelines: Category A and Category B ships should carry 20 unit-dose 'Minims' amethocaine 0.5% irrespective of crew size.

UK guidelines: Category A and Category B ships should carry 20 unit-dose 'Minims' tetracaine 0.5% for each 10 crew.

IMHA guidance: Category A ships should carry 20 single-use vials irrespective of crew size.

Shelf life: 24 months (unopened)

Recommendations:	Category A:	20 single-dose units irrespective of crew size
	Category B:	20 single-dose units irrespective of crew size
	Category C:	Nil

Amoxicillin/clavulanic acid (875mg/125mg) tablets

Indication(s): Bacterial infections, including – wound, skin, respiratory, and urinary tract infections; prostatitis; pelvic inflammatory disease

Dose(s): One tablet three times a day. Duration of therapy, usually 5–10 days for respiratory tract infections, up to 28 days for prostatitis

Existing recommendations:

Second edition: Not listed. The closest oral antibacterial recommended is ampicillin. However, this would not provide the cover for skin infections similar to amoxicillin/ clavulanic acid.

Australian guidelines: Not listed. The only oral antibacterials listed are erythromycin, doxycycline and ciprofloxacin; injectable benzylpenicillin and ceftriaxone are the only beta-lactam antibacterials listed.

UK guidelines: Not listed. The only oral antibacterials listed are erythromycin, doxycycline and ciprofloxacin; injectable benzylpenicillin and cefuroxime are the only beta-lactam antibacterials listed.

IMHA guidance: Category A ships should carry 15 tablets for 10 crew, 30 tablets for 20–30 crew, and 45 tablets for 40 crew.

Note: The range of indications for amoxicillin/clavulanic acid is wide, and includes conditions that are likely to be common on a ship (e.g. wounds).

Shelf life: 24–36 months

Recommendations:	Category A:	20 tablets per 10 crew
	Category B:	10 tablets per 10 crew
	Category C:	Nil

Artemether injection 80mg/ml

Indication(s): Management of severe (complicated) malaria

Dose(s): 3.2mg/kg initially then 1.6mg/kg daily until the patient can take oral artemether + lumefantrine

Existing recommendations:

Second edition: Not listed. Quinine injection and tablets are recommended for the treatment of malaria. The suggested holdings were 20 ampoules of quinine dihydrochloride injection 300mg/ml (600mg quinine dihydrochloride per 2-ml ampoule) for Category A ships, and Category B ships were not required to hold quinine. At the dose indicated in the second edition of the guide (600mg three times a day until the patient can take oral therapy) and assuming up to of 5 days of parenteral treatment, this quantity is sufficient to treat one patient.

Australian guidelines: Not listed. Mefloquine (60 tablets per 10 crew for Category A and 30 per 10 crew for Category B ships), pyrimethamine with sulfadoxine (12 tablets per 10 crew for Category A and B ships), and quinine tablets (50 tablets per 10 crew for Category A and

B ships) are recommended to treat malaria. These treatments are oral and would not be used for severe malaria.

UK guidelines: Not listed. Atovaquone with proguanil (Malarone™), quinine, doxycycline, mefloquine, co-artemether (artemether + lumefantrine) and chloroquine are all recommended for treatment. They are for oral treatment, and would not be used for severe malaria.

IMHA guidance: Category A ships should carry 5 ampoules irrespective of crew size.

Based on the recommended dose for an average 70kg adult, this would equate to 224mg initially (3 x 80mg/ml ampoules) followed by 112mg (2 x 80mg/ml ampoules) daily until the patient could take oral medication. Assuming it takes up to 4 days of subsequent parenteral therapy [10] the total amount of artemether needed would be 11 ampoules of 80mg/ml for a 70kg adult (assuming part ampoules are discarded); similarly, for a 100kg adult, 12 ampoules would be required.

Note: None of the treatments currently recommended in the Australian or UK guidelines are equivalent to the use of parenteral artemether. They are for oral treatment, and would be used for mild to moderate malaria.

Shelf life: 48 months[11]

Recommendations:	Category A:	12 ampoules irrespective of crew size
	Category B:	12 ampoules irrespective of crew size
	Category C:	Nil

Artemether + lumefantrine 20mg/120mg tablets

Indication(s): Treatment of malaria

Dose(s): The dose for an adult is 6-dose regimen of 4 tablets, given at specified intervals over 60 hours (total 24 tablets)

Existing recommendations:

Second edition: Not listed. Oral quinine is recommended for uncomplicated malaria (dose of two tablets three times a day for 7 days). The second edition suggested Category A ships carry 200 quinine 300mg tablets (equivalent to 50 to 70 tablets per 10 crew). This equates to approximately one or two treatment courses per 10 crew. Category B and C ships were not required to carry any quinine, but it was recommended that they carry 100 chloroquine 250mg tablets (approximately 50 per 10 crew), which could be used to treat malaria. It should be noted that the chloroquine was also recommended for prophylaxis and therefore the quantities that were recommended to be held do not reflect quantity for treatment alone.

Australian guidelines: Not listed. Mefloquine (60 tablets per 10 crew for Category A and 30 tablets per 10 crew for Category B ships), pyrimethamine with sulfadoxine (12 tablets per 10 crew for Category A and B ships), and quinine tablets (50 tablets per 10 crew for Category A and B ships) are recommended to treat mild to moderate malaria. The usual adult dose of pyrimethamine with sulfadoxine is 3 tablets as a single dose. The usual dose for quinine is 2 tablets 3 times daily for 7 days. The usual dose for mefloquine is 5 tablets as a single dose.

It should be noted that the Australian guidelines recommend mefloquine for prophylaxis as well as for the treatment of malaria. Therefore, the quantities recommended to be held do not represent that for treatment alone. The Australian guidelines suggest Category A and B ships carry enough pyrimethamine with sulfadoxine tablets to treat 4 people per 10 crew, and quinine to treat one person per 10 crew.

UK guidelines: Artemether + lumefantrine is recommended, along with atovaquone with proguanil (Malarone™), quinine, doxycycline, mefloquine, and chloroquine for mild to moderate malaria. The UK guidelines do not provide quantities, only a recommendation that 'appropriate emergency standby medication should also be carried'.[12]

IMHA guidance: Category A ships should carry 24 tablets for 10–20 crew, and 48 tablets for 30–40 crew.

Note: Artemether + lumefantrine is the only treatment available for mild to moderate malaria in the third edition of the guide. Double quantity if crew size exceeds 30.

Shelf life: 24 months

Recommendations:	Category A:	24 tablets irrespective of crew size
	Category B:	24 tablets irrespective of crew size
	Category C:	Nil

Atropine 1mg/ml (sulphate) injection

Indication(s): Management of slow heart rate (bradycardia) of myocardial infarction; treatment of organophosphate poisoning

Dose(s): Slow heart rate (bradycardia) of myocardial infarction: initial dose 500 micrograms, repeated every 3–5 minutes up to a maximum dose of 3mg

Organophosphate poisoning: 2mg, repeated every 10 to 30 minutes, if necessary, until muscarinic effects disappear or there are signs of atropine toxicity

Existing recommendations:

Second edition: Category A ships carry 60 ampoules (equivalent to 15–20 ampoules per 10 crew), and Category B ships carry 10 ampoules of atropine 500micrograms/ml (sulphate) injection, (equivalent to 5 ampoules per 10 crew for Category B ships).

Australian guidelines: Fifteen (15) ampoules for both Category A and Category B ships (listed under Section 15: Antidotes) to treat organophosphate poisoning (equivalent to 7.5 ampoules per 10 crew).

UK guidelines: Atropine is not listed except as part of a 'Doctors bag' to be carried by ships that have passengers.

IMHA guidance: Category A ships should carry 10 ampoules irrespective of crew size.

Shelf life: 36 months

Note: The recommended quantity should be doubled if cargo contains organophosphates.

Recommendations:	Category A:	10 ampoules irrespective of crew size
	Category B:	5 ampoules irrespective of crew size
	Category C:	Nil

Azithromycin 500mg tablets

Indication(s): Alternative to penicillin in patients with penicillin allergy; wounds; in combination with ceftriaxone for moderate/severe pneumonia and pelvic inflammatory disease (PID); ; in combination with ceftriaxone or ciprofloxacin in urethritis due to sexually transmitted infections (STIs); genital ulcer; impetigo; cholera; diphtheria; group A streptococcal (GAS) sore throat; typhoid; pertussis

Dose(s): Range from 1–2g (2–4 tablets) as a single dose for STIs; 500mg twice daily for 14 days for diphtheria (total 28 tablets); the most common dose is 500mg twice daily for 7–10 days or longer depending on the infection (e.g. 14 days for diphtheria).

Existing recommendations:

Second edition: Not listed. Erythromycin was the macrolide antibacterial recommended and it was suggested that Category A ships carry 300 erythromycin 250mg tablets (equivalent to approximately 75–100 per 10 crew) and Category B ships 100 erythromycin 250mg tablets (equivalent to 50 per 10 crew).

Australian guidelines: Not listed. Erythromycin was the macrolide antibacterial recommended and it was suggested that Category A ships carry 100 erythromycin 250mg tablets (50 tablets per 10 crew) and Category B ships, half this quantity (25 tablets per 10 crew).

UK guidelines: Not listed. Erythromycin was the macrolide antibacterial recommended and it was suggested that both Category A and Category B ships carry 28 erythromycin 250mg tablets per 10 crew.

IMHA guidance: Category A ships should carry 3 azithromycin 500mg tablets for 10–20 crew, and 6 azithromycin 500mg tablets for 30–40 crew.

Note: The standard dose of erythromycin for most indications is 250mg four times a day (4 tablets a day), and for azithromycin it is 500mg twice a day (two tablets per day). The likely major indications for azithromycin are going to be for sexually transmitted infections STIs), and pneumonia; for the treatment of pneumonia in a patient who is allergic to pencillin the duration would be up to 5 days (10 tablets).

Shelf life: 36 months

Recommendations:	Category A:	10 tablets irrespective of crew size
	Category B:	5 tablets irrespective of crew size
	Category C:	Nil

Ceftriaxone injection 1g (as sodium salt)

Indication(s): Third-generation cephalosporin antibacterial; shock as a result of severe infection; penetrating abdominal injuries; moderate to severe pneumonia; appendicitis; ulcerative colitis; jaundice; cholecystitis; septic abortion; puerperal sepsis; urethritis; pelvic inflammatory disease; cellulitis; septic arthritis; meningitis

Dose(s): For most indications, usual dose 1 to 2g daily as a single dose or in two divided doses; in severe infections up to 4g daily

Existing recommendations:

Second edition: Not listed. No cephalosporins were recommended and the only parenteral beta-lactam antibacterial was benzylpenicillin.

Australian guidelines: Category A ships should carry 20 ampoules (10 ampoules per 10 crew), and Category B ships are not required to carry ceftriaxone. However, it is recommended that Category B ships carry 5 ampoules of benzylpenicillin.

UK guidelines: Not listed. Category A ships are recommended to carry 20 ampoules cefuroxime (750mg/vial) per 10 crew; but Category B ships are not required to carry cefuroxime. However, it is suggested that Category B ships carry 2 ampoules of benzylpenicillin.

IMHA guidance: Category A ships should carry 15 ampoules per 10 crew.

Note: Ceftriaxone is the only parenteral /antibacterial listed in the third edition of the Guide.

Shelf life: 36 months

Recommendations:	Category A:	15 ampoules per 10 crew
	Category B:	5 ampoules irrespective of crew size
	Category C:	Nil

Cetirizine 10mg tablets

Indication(s): Pruritus; hay fever; scombroid fish poisoning; urticaria; anaphylaxis.

Dose(s): Usual dose 10mg once daily or 5mg twice daily.

Existing recommendations:

Second edition: Not listed. Chlorphenamine maleate was the only antihistamine recommended, and it was suggested that Category A ships carry 60 tablets (approximately 15–20 tablets per 10 crew), and Category B ships 20 tablets (10 tablets per 10 crew). The usual dose of chlorphenamine maleate is 4mg every 4–6 hours, maximum 24mg daily. Therefore, Category A ships carried approximately 5 to 7 days of treatment per 10 crew, and Category B 3 days treatment per 10 crew.

Australian guidelines: Not listed. Loratadine 10mg tablets is the only antihistamine listed, and Category A and B ships should carry 30 tablets irrespective of crew size. The recommended dose of loratadine is 10mg once daily.

UK guidelines: Category A and B ships should carry 30 cetirizine 10mg tablets irrespective of crew size.

IMHA guidance: Category A ships should carry 30 tablets irrespective of crew size.

Shelf life: 24 months

Recommendations:	Category A:	30 tablets irrespective of crew size
	Category B:	30 tablets irrespective of crew size
	Category C:	Nil

Charcoal, activated

Indication(s): Treatment of poisoning and drug overdose; reduces gastrointestinal absorption

Dose(s): Reduction of gastrointestinal absorption, 50 g

Existing recommendations:

Second edition: Category A, B and C ships should carry one bottle (120g) of activated charcoal powder.

Australian guidelines: Not listed. The Australian guidelines only recommend both Category A and Category B ships that carry dangerous goods should keep 200 activated charcoal 300mg tablets (60g).

UK guidelines: Not listed. There is no equivalent product recommended.

IMHA guidance: Category A ships should carry 100g (2x50g) irrespective of crew size.

Shelf life: 60 months

Recommendations:	Category A:	120g irrespective of crew size
	Category B:	120g irrespective of crew size
	Category C:	Nil

Ciprofloxacin 250mg tablets

Indication(s): Cat bite; gastroenteritis; heavy gastrointestinal haemorrhage; urinary tract infection; prostatitis; sexually transmitted infections (STIs); epididymitis; cellulitis from wounds received in seawater; anthrax; typhoid

Dose(s): The most common dose is 500–750mg twice a day; range 250–750mg twice daily. Duration of therapy ranges from a single dose (e.g. for gonorrhoea), to up to 28 days (e.g. prostatitis)

Existing recommendations:

Second edition: Not listed. There is no equivalent quinolone antibacterial recommended.

Australian guidelines: Category A ships should carry 28 tablets (approximately 7 to 10 tablets per 10 crew) and Category B ships 14 tablets.

UK guidelines: Category A ships should carry 20 tablets per 10 crew, and Category B ships 10 tablets per 10 crew. Double quantity if crew size exceeds 30.

IMHA guidance: Category A ships should carry 40 tablets irrespective of crew size.

Note: Should double the quantity if crew size is greater than 30.

Shelf life: 60 months

Recommendations:	Category A:	20 tablets irrespective of crew size
	Category B:	10 tablets irrespective of crew size
	Category C:	Nil

Cloves, oil of

Indication(s): Toothache

Dose(s): A few drops applied to the area

Existing recommendations:

Second edition: Category A ships should carry 40ml (approximately 10ml to 15ml per 10 crew) and Category B and C ships should carry 20ml (10ml per 10 crew).

Australian guidelines: Category A ships should carry 15ml (7.5ml per 10 crew) and Category B ships carry 15ml irrespective of crew size.

UK guidelines: Category A and Category B ships should carry 10ml irrespective of crew size.

IMHA guidance: Category A ships should carry 10ml irrespective of crew size.

Shelf life: not available

Recommendations:	Category A:	10ml per 10 crew
	Category B:	10ml irrespective of crew size
	Category C:	Nil

Dexamethasone injection 4mg/ml

Indication(s): Life-threatening and severe asthma; anaphylaxis; severe allergic reactions

Dose(s): Initially 0.4 to 20mg

Existing recommendations:

Second edition: Not listed. Hydrocortisone was included as an alternative parenteral steroid. Five (5) hydrocortisone 100mg ampoules recommended for Category A ships only (equivalent to approximately 2 ampoules per 10 crew). Hydrocortisone 100mg is equivalent to 4mg of dexamethasone.

Australian guidelines: Not listed. Parenteral hydrocortisone and oral prednisolone are included as alternative steroids. Five (5) 100mg hydrocortisone ampoules recommended for Category

A ships (equivalent to 2.5 ampoules per 10 crew), and 60 prednisolone 5mg tablets recommended for both Category A and Category B ships (equivalent to 30 tablets per 10 crew for Category A and Category B ships).

UK guidelines: Not listed. Parenteral hydrocortisone and oral prednisolone are included as alternative steroids. Three (3) hydrocortisone 100mg ampoules are recommended per 10 crew for Category A and 1 ampoule per 10 crew for Category B ships. Twenty eight (28) prednisolone 5mg tablets are recommended per 10 crew for both Category A and Category B ships.

IMHA guidance: Category A ships should carry 5 ampoules irrespective of crew size.

Note: Prednisone tablets are also listed in the third edition of the Guide.

Shelf Life: 24 months

Recommendations:	Category A:	3 ampoules per 10 crew
	Category B:	1 ampoule per 10 crew
	Category C:	Nil

Diazepam 5mg tablets

Indication(s): Alcohol withdrawal; psychosis (if patient remains agitated after haloperidol)

Dose(s): Ranges from 1 tablet as an immediate dose to 2 tablets every 6 hours (8 tablets per day)

Existing recommendations:

Second edition: Two hundred (200) 5 mg tablets recommended for Category A ships and 100 tablets for Category B ships (equivalent to approximately 50 tablets per 10 crew for Category A and Category B ships). Twenty (20) diazepam 2mg/ml ampoules are also listed for Category A ships (equivalent to 5 ampoules per 10 crew).

Australian guidelines: Forty (40) diazepam 5mg tablets recommended for Category A ships and 20 tablets for Category B ships irrespective of crew size. Two (2) diazepam 10mg/2ml ampoules also recommended irrespective of crew size.

UK guidelines: Twenty eight (28) diazepam 5mg tablets recommended for Category A ships only, irrespective of crew size. Five (5) diazepam 5mg/ml (2ml) ampoules also recommended irrespective of crew size.

IMHA guidance: Category A ships should carry 50 diazepam 5mg tablets for 10–20 crew, and 100 for 30–40 crew.

Note: Diazepam 5mg/ml (2ml) ampoules are not listed in the third edition of the guide. However, haloperidol injection is listed in the third edition of the Guide.

Shelf Life: 36 months

Recommendations:	Category A:	50 tablets irrespective of crew size
	Category B:	20 tablets irrespective of crew size
	Category C:	Nil

Docusate with senna tablets

Indication(s): Constipation; to avoid straining in patients with anal fissure and haemorrhoids

Dose(s): 1–2 tablets daily; up to 2 tablets twice daily

Existing recommendations:

Second edition: Not listed. No equivalent product listed.

Australian guidelines: Not listed. Glycerol suppositories are listed for this indication, with a suggested quantity of 12 suppositories for Category A ships (equivalent to 6 per 10 crew).

UK guidelines: Not listed. Glycerol suppositories are listed for this indication, with a suggested quantity of 12 suppositories per 10 crew for Category A ships.

IMHA guidance: Category A ships should carry 20 tablets for 10–20 crew, and 40 tablets for 30–40 crew.

Shelf Life: not available

Recommendations:	Category A:	30 tablets irrespective of crew size
	Category B:	Nil
	Category C:	Nil

Doxycycline 100mg tablets

Indication(s): Infections such as sexually transmitted infections (STIs); cellulitis; anthrax; plague.

Dose(s): 100mg twice daily for 5–10 days (depending on infection)

Existing recommendations:

Second edition: Two hundred (200) doxycycline 100mg tablets listed for Category A ships (equivalent to approximately 50–75 tablets per 10 crew).

Australian guidelines: Twenty one (21) doxycycline 100mg tablets recommended for Category A ships and 7 doxycycline 100mg tablets for Category B ships (equivalent to approximately 10 tablets per 10 crew for Category A).

UK guidelines: Eight (8) doxycycline 100mg capsules recommended for each 10 crew members for Category A ships.

IMHA guidance: Category A ships should carry 20 tablets for 10–20 crew, and 40 tablets for 30–40 crew.

Note: The third edition of the Guide also includes amoxicillin/clavulanate, which could be used for some of these indications.

Shelf Life: 48 months

Recommendations:	Category A:	10 tablets per 10 crew
	Category B:	Nil
	Category C:	Nil

Ethanol, hand cleanser gel 70%

Indication: Alternative to hand-washing when hands are not obviously soiled

Dose(s): not applicable

Existing recommendations:

Second edition: Not listed. Alcohol, rubbing (ethanol liquid) is listed for hand sanitization. Six 500ml bottles (3000ml) of Alcohol, rubbing (70% ethanol) listed for Category A ships and two 500ml bottles (1000ml) for Category B ships (equivalent to 750–1000ml per 10 crew for Category A ships and 500ml per 10 crew for Category B ships). The indication for rubbing alcohol also includes disinfecting instruments and surfaces.

Australian guidelines: Not listed.

UK guidelines: Not listed.

IMHA guidance: Category A ships should carry 500ml (2 x 250ml) per 10 crew.

Shelf Life: not available

Recommendations:	Category A:	500ml per 10 crew
	Category B:	500ml irrespective of crew size
	Category C:	100ml irrespective of crew size

Ethanol 70%, liquid

Indication: Disinfection of instruments and surfaces

Dose(s): Not applicable

Existing recommendations:

Second edition: Six 500ml bottles (3000ml) of Alcohol, rubbing (70% ethyl alcohol) listed for Category A ships and 2 x 500ml bottles (1000ml) for Category B ships (equivalent to 750–1000ml per 10 crew for Category A ships and 500ml per 10 crew for Category B ships). The indication also includes hand sanitization, but Ethanol hand cleanser gel 70% is now used. Category C ships were required to carry 500ml.

Australian guidelines: Not listed. One pack of 100 alcohol-impregnated swabs is recommended for each category of ship (equivalent to 50 swabs per 10 crew). The recommended disinfecting solution for instruments is chlorhexidine + cetrimide. It is suggested that Category A ships carry 24 x 100ml units, and Category B ships 12 x 100ml units, all irrespective of crew size.

UK guidelines: Not listed. One 100ml bottle or 1 pack of chlorhexidine + cetrimide impregnated wipes is recommended per 10 crew for Category A and Category B ships.

IMHA guidance: Category A ships should carry 500ml for 10–20 crew and 1000ml for 30–40 crew.

Shelf Life: not available

Recommendations:	Category A:	500ml per 10 crew
	Category B:	100ml per 10 crew
	Category C:	Nil

Fluorescein 1% eye strips

Indication(s): To detect damage to the cornea

Dose(s): Not applicable

Existing recommendations:

Second edition: One pack of 200 fluorescein strips listed for Category A ships only (equivalent to approximately 50–75 strips per 10 crew).

Australian guidelines: Twenty (20) individual disposable units (minims) recommended for both Category A and Category B ships (irrespective of crew size).

UK guidelines: Twenty (20) 0.5ml individual disposable units per 10 crew recommended for both Category A and Category B ships.

IMHA guidance: Category A ships should carry 20 strips irrespective of crew size.

Shelf Life: 15 months (unopened) – minims (individual units)

Recommendations:	Category A:	20 individual units irrespective of crew size
	Category B:	20 individual units irrespective of crew size
	Category C:	Nil

Furosemide injection: 40mg/4ml

Indication(s): Severe fluid retention in the lungs (pulmonary oedema) due to cardiac failure

Dose(s): 40mg, repeated in one hour if necessary

Existing recommendations:

Second edition: Not listed. One hundred (100) furosemide (frusemide) 40mg tablets listed for Category A ships only (equivalent to 25–30 tablets per 10 crew).

Australian guidelines: Five (5) furosemide 20mg/2ml ampoules recommended for Category A and Category B ships (equivalent to 2.5 ampoules per 10 crew = approximately 1 ampoule of 40mg/4ml furosemide per 10 crew). Twenty (20) furosemide 40mg tablets recommended for Category A ships only (irrespective of crew size).

UK guidelines: Two (2) furosemide 20mg/2ml ampoules per 10 crew for Category A ships only (equivalent to 1 ampoule of 40mg/4ml furosemide per 10 crew). Twenty eight (28) furosemide

40mg tablets recommended for both Category A and Category B ships (irrespective of crew size).

IMHA guidance: Category A ships should carry 5 furosemide 40mg/4ml ampoules irrespective of crew size.

Note: Furosemide tablets are not listed in the third edition of the Guide.

Shelf Life: 60 months

Recommendations:	Category A:	5 ampoules irrespective of crew size
	Category B:	5 ampoules irrespective of crew size
	Category C:	Nil

Glucagon injection 1mg

Indication(s): Hypoglycaemia

Dose(s): 1mg

Existing recommendations:

The second edition of the guide, and the Australian and UK guidelines do not provide quantities for glucagon ampoules.

IMHA guidance: Category A ships should carry one ampoule irrespective of crew size.

Shelf Life: 36 months (prior to reconstitution)

Recommendations:	Category A:	1 ampoule irrespective of crew size
	Category B:	1 ampoule irrespective of crew size
	Category C:	Nil

Haloperidol injection 5mg/ml

Indication(s): Severe psychotic hallucinations and delusions; severe agitation and aggressiveness

Dose(s): 2–10mg repeated every 2–6 hours if needed (maximum 15mg [3 ampoules] in 24 hours)

Existing recommendations:

Second edition: Not listed. Twenty (20) chlorpromazine 25mg/ml ampoules and 80 chlorpromazine 25mg tablets are recommended for Category A ships, (equivalent to 5–6 ampoules per 10 crew and 20–26 tablets per 10 crew). Ten (10) chlorpromazine 25mg ampoules and 40 chlorpromazine 25mg tablets are recommended for Category B ships (equivalent to 5 ampoules per 10 crew and 20 tablets per 10 crew). The recommended dose was up to 4 ampoules for delirium tremens, and up to 2 ampoules per day for other indications. Therefore, ships were recommended to carry approximately 1–2 days treatment per 10 crew.

Australian guidelines: Not listed. Ten (10) chlorpromazine 25mg/ml ampoules and 100 chlorpromazine 25mg tablets are recommended for Category A ships, irrespective of crew size. Five (5) chlorpromazine 25mg ampoules and 20 chlorpromazine 25mg tablets are recommended for Category B ships, irrespective of crew size.

UK guidelines: Not listed. Five (5) chlorpromazine 25mg ampoules per 10 crew and 28 chlorpromazine 25mg tablets per 10 crew is recommended for Category A ships. Twenty eight (28) chlorpromazine 25mg tablets per 10 crew is recommended for Category B ships, and no parenteral chlorpromazine listed.

IMHA guidance: Category A ships should carry 5 ampoules for 10–20 crew, and 10 ampoules for 30–40 crew.

Note: There are no oral antipsychotics listed in the third edition of the Guide. However, diazepam 5mg tablets are recommended.

Shelf Life: 60 months

Recommendations:	Category A:	5 ampoules per 10 crew
	Category B:	5 ampoules irrespective of crew size
	Category C:	Nil

Hydrocortisone 1% cream or ointment

Indication(s): Allergy and other inflammatory skin conditions

Dose(s): Apply sparingly twice per day

Existing recommendations:

Second edition: Six (6) hydrocortisone 1% ointment 30g (with rectal tip) tubes listed for Category A ships (equivalent to approximately 2 tubes per 10 crew for Category A) and 2 hydrocortisone 1% ointment 30g tubes for Category B and C ships (1 tube per 10 crew).

Australian guidelines: Two (2) hydrocortisone 1% cream or ointment 30g tubes (60g) recommended for Category A vessels (equivalent to 1 tube per 10 crew) and 1 x 30g tube for Category B vessels. [For hygiene reasons, each tube should only be used by one patient only.]

UK guidelines: Two (2) hydrocortisone 1% 15g cream tubes (30g) per 10 crew members for Category A ship and no stock listed for Category B ships.

IMHA guidance: Category A ships should carry 2 tubes (20g–30g) per 10 crew.

Shelf Life: 36 months

Recommendations:	Category A:	60g or 2 tubes per 10 crew
	Category B:	30g or 1 tube per 10 crew
	Category C:	Nil

Ibuprofen 400mg tablets

Indication(s): Inflammation; mild to moderate pain

Dose(s): 400–800mg every 6 hours (maximum 8 tablets per day)

Existing recommendations:

Second edition: Not listed. Acetylsalicylic acid was the only oral non-steroidal anti-inflammatory drug recommended. However, paracetamol also listed.

Australian guidelines: Forty eight (48) ibuprofen 200mg or 400mg tablets recommended for Category A ships and 24 ibuprofen 200mg or 400mg tablets recommended for Category B ships (equivalent to 12–16 tablets per 10 crew for Category A and 6–8 tablets per 10 crew for Category B ships). It should be noted that the Australian guide states that alternative non-steroidal anti-inflammatory drugs, including mefenamic acid or naproxen, could be stocked in place of ibuprofen. Five (5) diclofenac 50mg suppositories are also recommended per 10 crew for Category A ships only.

UK guidelines: One hundred (100) ibuprofen 400mg tablets per 10 crew recommended for Category A ships, and 50 ibuprofen 400mg tablets per 10 crew recommended for Category B and C ships. Ten diclofenac 50mg suppositories are also recommended per 10 crew for Category A ships only.

IMHA guidance: Category A ships should carry 50 tablets per 10 crew.

Note: The third edition lists acetylsalicylic acid and paracetamol, but no other non-steroidal anti-inflammatory drugs. Ibuprofen is considered a safer anti-inflammatory drug compared to aspirin, and is the usual first choice.

Shelf Life: 36 months

Recommendations:	Category A:	100 tablets per 10 crew
	Category B:	50 tablets per 10 crew
	Category C:	50 tablets irrespective of crew size

Isosorbide dinitrate 5mg (sublingual tablets)

Indication(s): Angina; myocardial infarction

Dose(s): one tablet, repeated after 10–15 minutes

Existing recommendations:

Second edition: Not listed. Forty (40) glyceryl trinitrate 0.5mg tablets recommended for this indication for Category A vessels and 20 glyceryl trinitrate 0.5mg tablets recommended for Category B and C vessels (equivalent to 10–15 tablets per 10 crew for Category A and approximately 5 tablets per 10 crew for Category B and C).

Australian guidelines: Not listed. Two (2) units of glyceryl trinitrate sublingual spray recommended for Category A vessels and 1 unit of glyceryl trinitrate sublingual spray recommended for Category B and C vessels (equivalent to 1 unit per 10 crew for Category A, B and C vessels).

UK guidelines: Not listed. One (1) unit of glyceryl trinitrate sublingual spray per 10 crew recommended for both Category A and Category B vessels. Glyceryl trinitrate transdermal patches (5mg x 2) are also listed, with 4 patches per 10 crew recommended for both Category A and Category B vessels.

IMHA guidance: Category A ships should carry 20 tablets for 10–20 crew, and 40 tablets for 30–40 crew.

Shelf Life: not available

Recommendations:	Category A:	10 tablets per 10 crew
	Category B:	10 tablets per 10 crew
	Category C:	5 tablets irrespective of crew size

Lidocaine injection 1% (50mg/5ml)

Indication(s): Local anaesthesia

Dose(s): Up to 200mg (4 ampoules)

Existing recommendations:

Second edition: Twelve (12) lidocaine (lignocaine) 2-ml ampoules recommended for Category A ships only. This is equivalent to 3–4 ampoules per 10 crew.

Australian guidelines: Twenty five (25) lidocaine 2-ml ampoules recommended for Category A and 5 lidocaine 2-ml ampoules recommended for Category B ships (equivalent to 12.5 x 2ml ampoules per 10 crew for Category A and 2.5 x 2ml ampoules per 10 crew for Category B ships = 5 x 5ml ampoules per 10 crew for Category A, and 1 x 5ml ampoule per 10 crew for Category B ships).

UK guidelines: Five (5) lidocaine 5-ml ampoules per 10 crew recommended for both Category A and Category B ships. One lidocaine gel 2% is also recommended for Category A ships only.

IMHA guidance: Category A ships should carry 5 ampoules for 10–20 crew, and 10 ampoules for 30–40 crew.

Note: The literature review indicates that minor injuries such as lacerations are common on ships.

Shelf Life: 48 months

Recommendations:	Category A:	5 ampoules per 10 crew
	Category B:	5 ampoules per 10 crew
	Category C:	Nil

Loperamide 2mg tablets

Indication(s): Diarrhoea

Dose(s): 2 tablets initially then 1 after each bowel motion; maximum of 8 tablets per 24 hours

Existing recommendations:

Second edition: Not listed. One hundred (100) codeine sulphate 30mg tablets recommended for both Category A and Category B ships (equivalent to approximately 25–30 tablets per 10 crew for Category A and 50 tablets per 10 crew for Category B ships). The recommend dose for diarrhoea was one tablet every four hours (6 tablets per day). Therefore, the recommended holding was for 4–5 days treatment per 10 crew for Category A and 8–10 days per 10 crew for Category B ships. If loperamide was used instead, this would equate to 32–40 tablets per 10 crew for Category A ships and 64–80 tablets per 10 crew for Category B ships.

Australian guidelines: Both loperamide 2mg capsules and codeine phosphate 30mg tablets are listed for this indication. For Category A ships, 24 loperamide 2mg capsules (equivalent to 12 capsules or 1.5 days of treatment per 10 crew) while for Category B ships, 16 capsules are recommended (equivalent to 8 capsules or one day of treatment per 10 crew).

UK guidelines: Thirty (30) loperamide 2mg capsules per 10 crew are recommended for Category A, B and C ships.

IMHA guidance: Category A ships should carry 30 tablets per 10 crew.

Note: Codeine sulphate 30mg tablets are not included in the third edition of the Guide.

Shelf Life: 60 months

Recommendations:	Category A:	30 tablets per 10 crew
	Category B:	30 tablets per 10 crew
	Category C:	10 tablets irrespective of crew size

Mebendazole 100mg tablets

Indication(s): Intestinal worm infections (not tapeworms)

Dose(s): 100mg once or twice daily for up to 3 days (pinworm, round worm, whipworm, hookworm)

300mg three times daily for 3 days then 500mg three times daily for 10 days (maximum dose of 177 tablets) (trichinellosis)

Existing recommendations:

Second edition: Not listed.

Australian guidelines: Six (6) mebendazole 100mg tablets recommended for both Category A and Category B ships, irrespective of crew size.

UK guidelines: Six (6) mebendazole 100mg tablets recommended for both Category A and Category B ships, irrespective of crew size.

IMHA guidance: Category A ships should carry 10 tablets for 10–20 crew and 20 tablets for 30–40 crew.

Note: Trichinellosis is an extremely rare intestinal worm infection; the most common worm infection is pinworm.

Shelf Life: 36 months

Recommendations:	Category A:	6 tablets, irrespective of crew size
	Category B:	6 tablets, irrespective of crew size
	Category C:	Nil

Metoprolol 100mg tablets

Indication(s): Hypertension; atrial fibrillation; angina pectoris; migraine prophylaxis

Dose(s): Hypertension: 100mg once daily

Atrial fibrillation, angina pectoris: 50mg twice daily, may be increased to 100mg twice daily

Migraine prophylaxis: 50mg twice daily

Existing recommendations:

Second edition: Not listed. No alternative product listed.

Australian guidelines: Not listed. Atenolol is listed as an antihypertensive agent and 28 atenolol 50mg tablets are recommended for Category A ships only (equivalent to approximately 14 per 10 crew).

UK guidelines: Not listed. Atenolol is listed as an antihypertensive agent and 28 atenolol 50mg tablets are recommended per 10 crew for Category A ships only.

IMHA guidance: Category A ships should carry 30 tablets for 10 crew, and 60 tablets for 20–40 crew.

Note: Atenolol is given once daily compared to metoprolol which is given twice daily (for most indications).

Shelf Life: 60 months

Recommendations:	Category A:	60 tablets irrespective of crew size
	Category B:	Nil
	Category C:	Nil

Metronidazole 500mg tablets

Indication(s): Ulcerative colitis; antibiotic associated colitis; jaundice; cholecystitis; trichomoniasis

Dose(s): Ulcerative colitis, jaundice, cholecystitis: 500mg 3 times daily
Antibiotic-associated colitis: 500mg 3 times daily for 10 days (15 doses)
Trichomoniasis: 2g (4 tablets) as a single dose

Existing recommendations:

Second edition: Five hundred (500) metronidazole 200mg tablets recommended for Category A ships (equivalent to 125–170 tablets per 10 crew). Two hundred (200) metronidazole 200mg tablets recommended for Category B ships (equivalent to 100 tablets per 10 crew).

Australian guidelines: Forty two (42) metronidazole 400mg tablets recommended for Category A ships (equivalent to 21 tablets per 10 crew) and 21 metronidazole 400mg tablets for Category B ships (equivalent to approximately 10 tablets per 10 crew). Twenty (20) metronidazole 1g suppositories also listed for Category A ships only (equivalent to 10 suppositories per 10 crew). Twenty four (24) tinidazole 500mg tablets are also recommended for Category A ships (equivalent to 12 tablets per 10 crew) and 12 tinidazole 500mg tablets recommended for Category B ships (equivalent to 6 tablets per 10 crew).

UK guidelines: Twenty one (21) metronidazole 400mg or 500mg tablets recommended per 10 crew for both Category A and Category B ships. Ten (10) metronidazole 1g suppositories also recommended per 10 crew for Category A ships only.

IMHA guidance: Category A ships should carry 30 tablets irrespective of crew size.

Note: Metronidazole suppositories and tinidazole tablets are not included in the third edition of the Guide.

Shelf Life: 60 months

Recommendations:	Category A:	30 tablets irrespective of crew size
	Category B:	20 tablets irrespective of crew size
	Category C:	Nil

Miconazole cream 2%

Indication(s): Topical antifungal

Dose(s): Apply twice daily, continuing for 2 weeks after symptoms resolve

Existing recommendations:

Second edition: Not listed. Five (5) miconazole 2% vaginal creams (80g with applicator) were recommended for Category A ships (equivalent to 1 to 2 treatments per 10 crew, as each unit is only used for one patient) while 2 were recommended for Category B ships (equivalent to 1 treatment per 10 crew). 20 miconazole 100mg pessaries were recommended for Category A ships, and 10 miconazole 100mg pessaries for Category B ships (equivalent to 5–6 pessaries per 10 crew for Category A and 5 pessaries per 10 crew for Category B ships).

Australian guidelines: Two (2) 30g tubes of miconazole 2% topical cream are recommended for Category A ships (equivalent to 1 treatment per 10 crew) and 1 tube is recommended for Category B ships (equivalent to 1 treatment per 10 crew). One 100g unit of benzoic acid compound ointment is recommended for Category A ships only (equivalent to 1 treatment per 10 crew as each unit should be only used for one patient). Two (2) miconazole 2% vaginal cream (40g with applicator) and 2 packs of 7 miconazole 100mg pessaries are also recommended for Category A ships and one tube of vaginal cream for Category B ships.

UK guidelines: Two (2) individual 30g tubes of miconazole 2% topical cream recommended for Category A ships (equivalent to 2 treatments per 10 crew) and 1 individual 30g tube of miconazole 2% topical cream for Category B ships (1 treatment per 10). Three (3) 15g units of benzoic acid compound ointment are recommended for Category A ships (equivalent to 3 per 10 crew) and 1 unit per 10 crew for Category B ships. If women are on board it is also recommended to stock 2 clotrimazole 500mg pessaries for Category A ships (equivalent to 2 treatments per 10 crew) and 1 for Category B ships (equivalent to 1 treatment to 10 crew).

IMHA guidance: Category A ships should carry 2 tubes of miconazole 2% cream per 10 crew.

Note: There are no specific vaginal preparations listed in the third edition of the guide. Quantities should be doubled if women are on board the ship.

Shelf Life: 24 months

Recommendations:	Category A:	2 x 30g tube per 10 crew
	Category B:	1 x 30g tube per 10 crew
	Category C:	Nil

Midazolam injection 5mg/ml

Indication(s): Seizures (epileptic fits); alternative to haloperidol for sedation of violent patients

Dose(s): 0.1–0.2 mg/kg (approximately 10–15mg) IM or 10mg intranasally

Existing recommendations:

Second edition: Not listed. Twenty (20) ampoules diazepam injection 10mg/ml were recommended for Category A ships only (equivalent to approximately 5–7 ampoules per 10 crew). The maximum recommended dose of diazepam for seizures is 50mg (or 5 ampoules) over 60 minutes. Therefore Category A ships would carry enough to treat approximately one patient at maximum doses per 10 crew.

Australian guidelines: Not listed. Five (5) diazepam rectal 10mg preparations are recommended for both Category A and Category B ships. The maximum dose is 10mg. Therefore this is equivalent to 2.5 treatments per 10 crew.

UK guidelines: Not listed. Five (5) diazepam rectal 10mg preparations are recommended for both Category A and Category B vessels. The maximum dose is 10mg. Therefore this is equivalent to 5 treatments per 10 crew.

IMHA guidance: Category A ships should carry 5 ampoules for 10–20 crew, and 10 ampoules for 30–40 crew.

Note: Based on the recommended doses in the third edition of the guide, up to 3 ampoules would be used for one patient with a seizure.

Shelf Life: 36 months

Recommendations:	Category A:	10 ampoules irrespective of crew size
	Category B:	5 ampoules irrespective of crew size
	Category C:	Nil

Misoprostol 200microgram tablets

Indication(s): Prevention of post-partum haemorrhage

Dose(s): 600 micrograms (3 tablets) immediately after delivery

Existing recommendations:

The second edition of the Guide, and the Australian and UK guidelines do not provide quantities for misoprostol tablets.

IMHA guidance: Category A ships should carry 3 tablets irrespective of crew size.

Note: Given the indication, this is only required if females are on board the ship.

Shelf Life: 36 months

Recommendations:	Category A:	3 tablets, irrespective of crew size
	Category B:	3 tablets, irrespective of crew size
	Category C:	Nil

Morphine ampoules 10mg/ml

Indication(s): severe pain and pain not responsive to other analgesics

Dose(s): 2.5mg–12.5mg every two hours dependent on age

Existing recommendations:

Second edition: Twenty (20) ampoules for Category A ships (equivalent to 2–3 ampoules per 10 crew), and 10 ampoules for Category B ships (equivalent to 2.5 ampoules per 10 crew).

Australian guidelines: Ten (10) ampoules for Category A ships (equivalent to 5 ampoules per 10 crew), and 5 ampoules for Category B ships (equivalent to 2.5 ampoules per 10 crew).

UK guidelines: Ten (10) ampoules per 10 crew for Category A and Category B ships

IMHA guidance: Category A ships should carry 10 ampoules for every 10 crew.

Shelf Life: 36 months

Recommendations:	Category A:	10 ampoules per 10 crew
	Category B:	10 ampoules per 10 crew
	Category C:	Nil

Morphine liquid 1mg/ml

Indication(s): severe pain in patients able to eat or drink

Dose(s): 3.75mg–18.75mg every two hours dependent on age

Existing recommendations:

Second edition: Not listed. No equivalent recommended.

Australian guidelines: Not listed. Codeine phosphate 30mg recommended. Sixty (60) tablets for Category A ships (equivalent to 30 tablets per 10 crew; equivalent to 112ml of morphine 1mg/ml liquid per 10 crew), 30 tablets for Category B ships (equivalent to 15 tablets per 10 crew; equivalent to 60ml of morphine 1mg/ml liquid per 10 crew), and 20 tablets for Category C ships (equivalent to 10 tablets per 10 crew; equivalent to 37.5ml of morphine 1mg/ml liquid per 10 crew)

UK guidelines: Not listed. Codeine phosphate 30mg recommended. Twenty-eight (28) tablets per 10 crew for both Category A and Category B ships (equivalent to 105ml of morphine 1mg/ml liquid per 10 crew).

IMHA guidance: Category A ships should carry 100ml of morphine 1mg/ml liquid irrespective of crew size.

Notes: Codeine is also used for diarrhoea in the Australian Guidelines. The conversion between codeine and morphine was 240mg of oral codeine being equivalent to 30mg of oral morphine. Therefore, each 30mg tablet of codeine is approximately equivalent 3.75ml of morphine 1mg/ml liquid. Double quantity if crew size exceeds 30.

Shelf Life: 36 months – opened containers must be used in 3 months

Recommendations:	Category A:	100ml irrespective of crew size
	Category B:	100ml irrespective of crew size
	Category C:	Nil

Naloxone ampoules 0.4mg/ml

Indication(s): reverse the effects of opiates, particularly in overdose

Dose(s): 0.4mg, repeated as needed

Existing recommendations:

Second edition: Six (6) ampoules for Category A ships only (equivalent to 1 to 2 ampoules per 10 crew).

Australian guidelines: Five (5) ampoules for both Category A and B ships (equivalent to 2.5 ampoules per 10 crew)

UK guidelines: Not listed. No equivalent recommended.

IMHA guidance: Category A ships should carry 10 ampoules irrespective of crew size.

Shelf Life: 36 months

Recommendations:	Category A:	10 ampoules irrespective of crew size
	Category B:	5 ampoules irrespective of crew size
	Category C:	Nil

Omeprazole tablets 20mg

Indication(s): Gastro-oesophageal reflux and peptic ulcer disease

Dose(s): 20mg daily; increase to 40mg if needed

Existing recommendations:

Second edition: Not listed. Only simple antacids recommended.

Australian guidelines: Not listed. Cimetidine 400mg tablets recommended. Sixty (60) tablets for Category A ships only (equivalent to 30 tablets per 10 crew; equivalent to 15 days treatment per 10 crew).

UK guidelines: Not listed. Cimetidine 400mg tablets recommended. Sixty (60) tablets for Category A ships only (equivalent to 30 days treatment per 10 crew).

IMHA guidance: Category A ships should carry 30 omeprazole 20mg tablets for 10–20 crew, and 60 omeprazole 20mg tablets for 30–40 crew.

Notes: The daily treatment dose of cimetidine was assumed to be 800mg per day. No other antacid is listed in the 3rd edition of the Guide. Double quantity if crew size exceeds 30.

Shelf Life: 36 months

Recommendations:	Category A:	30 tablets irrespective of crew size
	Category B:	30 tablets irrespective of crew size
	Category C:	Nil

Ondansetron tablets 4mg

Indication(s): prevent vomiting and sea-sickness

Dose(s): one tablet before the stimulus to vomit

Existing recommendations:

Second edition: Not listed. Cyclizine 50mg tablets listed. Four-hundred (400) tablets for Category A ships (equivalent to 100–130 tablets per 10 crew), and 100 tablets for Category B and C ships (equivalent to 50 tablets per 10 crew).

Australian guidelines: Not listed. Prochlorperazine 5mg tablets recommended. Twenty-five (25) tablets for Category A and B ships irrespective of crew size.

UK guidelines: Not listed. Prochlorperazine 3mg buccal tablets recommended. Fifty (50) tablets for Category A and B ships irrespective of crew size.

IMHA guidance: Category A ships should carry 10 ondansetron 4mg tablets for 10–20 crew, and 20 ondansetron 4mg tablets for 30–40 crew.

Notes: No other anti-emetics are listed in the 3rd edition of the Guide

Shelf Life: 36 months

Recommendations:	Category A:	10 tablets per 10 crew
	Category B:	10 tablets per 10 crew
	Category C:	10 tablets irrespective of crew size

Oral Rehydration Salts (ORS) sachets

Indication(s): Prevention and treatment of dehydration, especially due to diarrhoea

Dose(s): Sachets are to be reconstituted with the appropriate volume of boiled, cooled water and taken according to recommendations (1 cup i.e., 250 ml, for each diarrhoeal stool associated with infectious diseases for mild dehydration; every hour for the first four hours for moderate dehydration)

Existing recommendations:

Second edition: Fifty (50) bags/sachets (each to be dissolved in 1000ml, solution is stable for 24 hours) for Category A ships and 20 bags/sachets for Category B ships. As each bag/sachet is made up to 1000ml treatments, this is equivalent to 50l for Category A and 20l for Category B ships (equivalent to 12–15l per 10 crew for Category A and 10l per 10 crew for Category B). Category C vessels hold 5l.

Australian guidelines: One hundred and twenty (120) sachets per 20 crew are held for Category A ships and 40 sachets are held for Category B ships. Each sachet is designed to be dissolved in 200ml. Therefore Category A ships carry the equivalent of 24l and Category B 8l (equivalent to 12l per 10 crew for Category A and 4l per 10 crew for Category B).

UK guidelines: 16–20 sachets per 10 crew for both Category A and B ships. Each sachet is designed to be dissolved in 1l of water. Therefore both Category A and Category B ships carry 16–20l per 10 crew.

IMHA guidance: Category A ships should carry 10 sachets for 10–20 crew, and 20 sachets for 30–40 crew; the volume that the sachets produce is not stated. It is assumed that each makes 1l.

Note: For commercial preparations such as Gastrolyte®, each sachet is to be mixed with 200ml of water. Therefore 75 sachets would be required for 15l of oral rehydration solution, 50 sachets for 10l and 10 sachets for 2l.

Shelf Life: 24 months (Dioralyte®)

Recommendations:	Category A:	15l per 10 crew
	Category B:	10l per 10 crew
	Category C:	2l irrespective of crew size

Oxymetazoline 0.5% nasal drops (or equivalent vasoconstrictor spray or drops)

Indication(s): Nasal obstruction due to allergies or viral infection, or to improve sinus drainage in sinusitis.

Dose(s): 2–3 drops in each nostril twice daily or at night if disturbed sleep is the main complaint. [An individual dose unit should be used for each patient for hygiene reasons.]

Existing recommendations:

Second edition: Not listed. Category A ships recommended to hold 100 ephedrine 25mg tablets (equivalent to 25–30 tablets per 10 crew), and Category B ships were not required to carry any ephedrine tablets. At the recommended dose (one tablet four times a day) this would equate to 5–6 days treatment per 10 crew for Category A ships only.

Australian guidelines: Not listed. Ephedrine 0.5% nasal drops BP; 2 units for Category A ships and 1 unit for Category B ships, irrespective of crew size. Category A ships are recommended to carry 120 generic 'cold and flu' tablets, which would contain an oral decongestant (equivalent to 30–40 tablets per 10 crew = 6–10 days treatment per 10 crew). Category B ships were not required to carry any 'cold and flu' tablets.

UK guidelines: Not listed. Ephedrine 0.5% nasal drops; 1 unit for Category A and Category B ships, irrespective of crew size. Category A and B ships were recommended to carry proprietary cold remedy 'as required'

IMHA guidance: Category A ships should carry 4 units for 10 crew, and one additional unit for each additional 10 crew above 10 (e.g. 5 units for 20 crew, 6 units for 30 crew).

Note: The third edition does not recommend any oral decongestant agent.

Shelf Life: 36 months

Recommendations:	Category A:	2 units per 10 crew
	Category B:	1 unit per 10 crew
	Category C:	Nil

Paracetamol 500mg tablets

Indication(s): Pain and fever

Dose(s): Two tablets (1g) four times a day (maximum 8 tablets per day)

Existing recommendations:

Second edition: Category A ships should carry 300 tablets (approximately 70 to 100 tablets per 10 crew) and Category B ships 150 tablets (75 tablets per 10 crew). Category C ships were required to carry 100 tablets.

Australian guidelines: Category A and Category B ships should carry 500 tablets (250 tablets per 10 crew). Category C ships were required to carry 50 tablets.

UK guidelines: Category A ships should carry 100 tablets per 10 crew and Category B and C ships 50 tablets per 10 crew.

IMHA guidance: Category A ships should carry 100 tablets per 10 crew.

Shelf life: 36–60 months

Recommendations:	Category A:	100 tablets per 10 crew
	Category B:	50 tablets per 10 crew
	Category C:	25 tablets per 10 crew

Permethrin 1% lotion

Indication(s): Hair, pubic and body lice

Dose(s): Apply to the hair and keep in contact for 5 minutes then rinse; treat all close contacts

Existing recommendations:

Second edition: Not listed. The alternative product listed is lindane cream. The recommended holding was 12 x 60g tubes for Category A ships, and 2 x 60g tubes for Category B ships (approximately 3 to 4 tubes per 10 crew for Category A, and 1 tube per 10 crew for Category B ships). Lindane also recommended for the treatment of scabies.

Australian guidelines: Category A ships should carry 200ml of permethrin 1% hair application irrespective of crew size, and there was no recommended holding for Category B ships.

UK guidelines: Category A ships should carry two bottles of permethrin 1% crème rinse irrespective of crew size, and there was no recommended holding for Category B ships.

IMHA guidance: Category A ships should carry 250ml for 10–20 crew, and 500ml for 30–40 crew.

Note: The third edition of the guide recommends separate treatment for head lice and scabies. Double quantity if crew size exceeds 30.

Shelf life: 24 months

Recommendations:	Category A:	200ml irrespective of crew size
	Category B:	100ml irrespective of crew size
	Category C:	Nil

Permethrin 5% lotion

Indication(s): Scabies

Dose(s): Apply to the entire body from the neck down and leave on for 8–12 hours before rinsing

Existing recommendations:

Second edition: Not listed. The alternative product listed is lindane cream. The recommended holding was 12 x 60g tubes for Category A ships, and 2 x 60g tubes for Category B ship (approximately 3 to 4 tubes per 10 crew for Category A, which equates to 3–4 treatments per

10 crew and 1 tube per 10 crew for Category; one treatment per 10 crew). Lindane was also suggested for the treatment of head lice.

Australian guidelines: Category A ships should carry 6 x 30g tubes of permethrin 5% cream (3 x 30g tubes per 10 crew = 3 treatments per 10 crew). Category B ships were recommended to carry 2 x 30g (1 tube per 10 crew; 1 treatment per 10 crew) of permethrin 5%.

UK guidelines: There is no recommendation to carry the 5% lotion for either Category A or Category B ships.

IMHA guidance: Category A ships should carry 250g for 10–20 crew, and 500g for 30–40 crew.

Note: Australian pack sizes (Quellada®) are 100ml for the treatment of one adult.

Shelf life: not available

Recommendations:	Category A:	300ml irrespective of crew size
	Category B:	100ml irrespective of crew size
	Category C:	Nil

Povidone iodine 10% solution

Indication(s): Disinection of skin and wounds

Dose(s): Not applicable

Existing recommendations:

Second edition: Not listed. The recommended skin disinfectant was iodine solution. It was recommended that Category A ships carry 400ml and Category B ships 200ml (approximately 100–150ml per 10 crew for Category A and 100ml per 10 crew for Category B). Category C ships were required to carry 100ml.

Australian guidelines: Not listed. The recommended disinfectant is cetrimide + chlorhexidine solution. The recommended holding of this is 2400ml for Category A ships, and 1200ml for Category B ships irrespective of crew size.

UK guidelines: Not listed. The recommended disinfectant is cetrimide + chlorhexidine solution. The recommended holding of this is 100ml for Category A and Category B ships irrespective of crew size.

IMHA guidance: Category A ships should carry 2 bottles (30ml–120ml) per 10 crew, and one additional bottle for every 10 crew over 10 (e.g. 3 bottles for 20 crew, 4 for 30 crew).

Note: Povidone iodine should be used sparingly and is generally not recommended by most wound specialists.

Shelf life: 36 months (unopened)

Recommendations:	Category A:	100ml per 10 crew
	Category B:	100ml per 10 crew
	Category C:	100ml irrespective of crew size

Povidone iodine 10% ointment

Indication(s): Minor wounds

Dose(s): Not applicable

Existing recommendations:

Second edition: Not listed. There are no alternative antiseptic ointments recommended.

Australian guidelines: Not listed. Silver sulfadiazine cream is recommended for the treatment of burns.

UK guidelines: Not listed. Silver sulfadiazine cream is recommended for the treatment of burns.

IMHA guidance: Category A ships should carry 2 tubes for 10 crew and one additional tube for every additional 10 crew (e.g 3 tubes for 20 crew, 4 for 30 crew).

Note: Povidone iodine should be used sparingly and is generally not recommended by most wound specialists.

Shelf life: 36 months (unopened)

Recommendations:	Category A:	one tube (25g) irrespective of crew size
	Category B:	one tube (25g) irrespective of crew size
	Category C:	Nil

Prednisone 25mg tablets

Indication(s): Acute asthma attack; severe inflammatory reactions

Dose(s): Usual dose 25mg to 50mg per day

Existing recommendations:

Second edition: Not listed. The recommended steroid for acute asthma and severe inflammation was hydrocortisone injection.

Australian guidelines: Not listed. Category A and B ships to carry 60 prednisone 5mg tablets (30 x 5mg tablets per 10 crew, equivalent to 6 x 25mg tablets per 10 crew).

UK guidelines: Not listed. Category A and B ships to carry 28 x 5mg tablets per 10 crew. This is equivalent to approximately 6 x 25mg per 10 crew.

IMHA guidance: Category A ships should carry 30 tablets for 10–20 crew and 60 tablets for 30–40 crew.

Note: Dexamethasone injection is also listed in the third edition of the Guide to treat severe asthma and inflammatory conditions.

Shelf life: 36–60 months

Recommendations:	Category A:	30 tablets irrespective of crew size
	Category B:	30 tablets irrespective of crew size
	Category C:	Nil

Salbutamol inhaler 100ug/dose (200 doses per inhaler)

Indication(s): Acute asthma and anaphylaxis

Dose(s): Awo to four doses via spacer repeated every 10 minutes if necessary.

Existing recommendations:

Second edition: Category A ships should carry two inhalers and Category B one inhaler (approximately one inhaler per 10 crew for Category A).

Australian guidelines: Category A ships should carry two inhalers and Category B ships one inhaler (one inhaler per 10 crew for Category A).

UK guidelines: Category A and B ships to carry one inhaler per 10 crew.

IMHA guidance: Category A ships should carry one inhaler per 10 crew.

Shelf life: 36 months

Recommendations:	Category A:	one inhaler per 10 crew
	Category B:	one inhaler per 10 crew
	Category C:	Nil

Sodium chloride 0.9% infusion, 1 Litre

Indication(s): Fluid replacement

Dose(s): Not applicable

Existing recommendations:

Second edition: Category A ships should carry 6 x 1litre and Category B ships 2 x 1litre (approximately 2litre per 10 crew for Category A and 1litre per 10 crew for Category B ships).

Australian guidelines: Category A ships carry 5 x 1litre and Category B ships 3 x 1litre (approximately 2litre per 10 crew for Category A and B ships). [Only recommended for ships that carry hazardous materials.]

UK guidelines: Not listed.

IMHA guidance: Category A ships should carry 5 x 1litre infusions irrespective of crew size.

Shelf life: not available

Recommendations:	Category A:	5 x 1litre irrespective of crew size
	Category B:	1 x 1litre per 10 crew
	Category C:	Nil

Tetracycline eye ointment

Indication(s): Eye and ear infections

Dose(s): Applied to the eye every 4 to 6 hours; 5g instilled into the ear canal

Existing recommendations:

Second edition: Category A ships should hold 6 tubes and Category B ships 3 tubes (approximately 2 tubes per 10 crew for Category A and B). Category C ships were required to carry 1 tube.

Australian guidelines: Not listed. The alternative antibiotic eye ointment recommended is framycetin eye ointment. Category A ships carry 5 tubes and Category B carry 2 tubes (approximately 2 tubes per 10 crew for Category A ships, and one tube per 10 crew for Category B ships).

UK guidelines: Not listed. The alternative antibiotic eye ointment recommended is chloramphenicol eye ointment. Category A ships carry 4 tubes per 10 crew and Category B ships carry 1 tube per 10 crew.

IMHA guidance: Category A ships should carry 2 tubes per 10 crew.

Note: Both the Australian and UK guidelines also list antibiotic eye drops and antibiotic ear drops; the third edition of the guide does not include any other treatments for eye or ear infections.

Shelf life: not available

Recommendations:	Category A:	2 tubes per 10 crew
	Category B:	1 tube per 10 crew
	Category C:	1 tube irrespective of crew size

Vitamin K injection 10mg/ml

Indication(s): Reverse unwanted effects of warfarin or similar drugs (e.g. rat poison)

Dose(s): 10mg subcutaneously

Existing recommendations:

Second edition: Not listed.

Australian guidelines: Only lists vitamin K for paediatric use (one ampoule per ship regardless of crew size) and for ships carrying hazardous cargo: 10 ampoules for Category A ships only (equivalent of 5 ampoules per 10 crew).

UK guidelines: Only lists vitamin K for paediatric use (one ampoule per ship regardless of crew size).

IMHA guidance: Category A ships should carry 2 ampoules irrespective of crew size.

Shelf life: 36 months

Recommendations:	Category A:	2 ampoules irrespective of crew size
	Category B:	2 ampoules irrespective of crew size
	Category C:	Nil

Water for injection

Indication(s): Reconstituting parenteral medications

Dose(s): Not applicable

Existing recommendations:

Second edition: Category A ships hold 30 x 5ml ampoules, and Category B ships 20 x 5ml ampoules (equivalent to 5–10 ampoules per 10 crew for Category A and 10 ampoules per 10 crew for Category B ships).

Australian guidelines: Water for injection listed to reconstitute benzylpenicillin injections. Twenty (20) ampoules for Category A ships, and 5 ampoules for Category B ships (equivalent to 10 ampoules per 10 crew for Category A ships).

UK guidelines: Not listed.

IMHA guidance: Category A ships should carry 20 ampoules for 10 crew, and an additional 10 ampoules for each 10 crew over 10 (e.g. 30 ampoules for 20 crew, 40 for 30 crew).

Note: The only injection requiring water for injection in the third edition of the Guide is ceftriaxone.

Shelf life: not available

Recommendations:	Category A:	10 ampoules per 10 crew
	Category B:	5 ampoules irrespective of crew size
	Category C:	Nil

Zidovudine plus lamivudine 300mg/150mg tablets

Indication(s): Prophylaxis against HIV after needle-stick injury

Dose(s): One tablet twice a day for four weeks (56 tablets per course)

Existing recommendations:

The second edition of the Guide and the Australian and UK guidelines do not provide quantities for zidovudine plus lamivudine tablets. No equivalent product listed.

IMHA guidance: Category A ships should carry at least 60 zidovudine plus lamivudine tablets.

Note: According to the third edition of the Guide, HIV prophylaxis is not required for all needle-stick injuries and the treatment course would be stopped if a negative blood result for HIV is obtained.

Shelf life: 24 months

Recommendations:	Category A:	56 tablets irrespective of crew size
	Category B:	56 tablets irrespective of crew size
	Category C:	Nil

Zinc oxide paste/ointment

Indication(s): Protect irritated skin (e.g. anal pruritus)

Dose(s): Not applicable

Existing recommendations:

Second edition: Category A ships hold 12 x 30g tubes and Category B and C ships, 3 x 30g tubes (equivalent to 3–4 tubes [90g–120g] per 10 crew for Category A ships and 1–2 tubes [30g–60g] per 10 crew for Category B and C ships).

Australian guidelines: Category A and Category B ships should keep 1 x 100g unit irrespective of crew size.

UK guidelines: Category A ships should keep 1 x 25g tube of zinc oxide ointment irrespective of crew size, and Category B ships are not required to keep zinc oxide ointment.

IMHA guidance: Category A ships should carry 5 tubes/tubs (50g–100g) irrespective of crew size.

Shelf life: not available

Recommendations:	Category A:	200g irrespective of crew size
	Category B:	100g irrespective of crew size
	Category C:	100g irrespective of crew size

Acknowledgements: This text was prepared in December 2009 by David Newby and Felicity Prior at the University of Newcastle WHO Collaborating Centre for Training in Pharmacoeconomics and Rational Pharmacotherapy, Waratah, New South Wales, Australia.

Conflicts-of-interest: Neither author has declared any conflicts-of-interest.

Review-by date: Based on feedback received from users of this quantification addendum, WHO plans to incorporate a quantification list in the fourth edition of the *International Medical Guide for Ships*, scheduled for publication in 2012.

Annex 1: Mapping of the medicines in the third edition of the Guide to the quantities in the second edition

Name	Form[a]	Strength	Indication[b]	second edition of the Guide[c]			Notes on the second edition of the Guide[d]
				A	B	C	
Acetylsalicylic acid	tab	300mg	Pain, fever, blood clots	600	300	200	No other anti-inflammatories
Aciclovir	tab	400mg	Herpes simplex/zoster	-	-	-	No equivalent recommended
Adrenaline	amp	1mg/ml	Anaphylaxis	20	10	10	Epinephrine
Amoxicillin/ clavulanic acid	tab	875mg/125mg	Infections	-	-	-	Ampicillin only oral beta-lactam
Artemether	amp	80mg/ml	Malaria treatment	20*	-	-	Quinine 600mg injection
Artemether + lumefantrine	tab	20mg/120mg	Malaria treatment	200*	100*	100*	Quinine tablets (A); chloroquine (B/C)
Atropine	amp	1.2mg/ml	MI/organophosphate poisoning	60	10	-	0.5mg/ml
Azithromycin	tab	500mg	Infections	300*	100*	-	Erythromycin only macrolide
Ceftriaxone	amp	1g	Infections	-	-	-	Benzyl penicillin only
Cetirizine	tab	10mg	Hayfever/hives/dermatitis	60*	20*	-	Chlorphenamine 4mg tablets
Charcoal, activated	powder		Poisoning	120g	120g	120g	
Ciprofloxacin	tab	250mg	Infections	-	-	-	No equivalent recommended
Cloves, oil of	liq		Toothache	40ml	20ml	20ml	
Dexamethasone	amp	4mg/ml	Severe asthma/ anaphylaxis	5*	-	-	Hydrocortisone 100mg amp
Diazepam	tab	5mg	Alcohol withdrawal	200	100	-	
Docusate with senna	tab	50mg/8mg	Constipation	-	-	-	No equivalent recommended
Doxycycline	tab	100mg	Infections	200	-	-	
Ethanol, hand cleanser	gel	70%	Hand cleaning	-	-	-	Ethanol liquid only

Name	Form[a]	Strength	Indication[b]	second edition of the Guide[c]			Notes on the second edition of the Guide[d]
				A	B	C	
Ethanol	liq	70%	Disinfect instruments	3000ml	1000ml	500ml	For hand sanitization also
Fluorescein	eye strips	1%	Detect corneal damage	200	-	-	
Frusemide	amp	40mg/4ml	Pulmonary oedema	-	-	-	Frusemide 40mg tablets only (A)
Glucagon	amp	1mg	Hypoglycaemia	-	-	-	No equivalent recommended
Haloperidol	amp	5mg/ml	Psychosis/severe agitation	20*	10*	-	Chlorpromazine 25mg/ml
Hydrocortisone	crm	1%	Allergy/inflammatory skin	6*	2*	2*	Ointment; also for rectal use
Ibuprofen	tab	400mg	Inflammation/pain	-	-	-	Aspirin only NSAID
Isosorbide dinitrate	tab	5mg	Angina/MI	40*	20*	20*	Glyceryl trinitrate
Lignocaine	amp	1%, 5ml	Suturing/minor surgery	12	-	-	
Loperamide	tab	2mg	Diarrhoea	100*	100*	-	Codeine 30mg tabs; also for cough
Mebendazole	tab	100mg	Intestinal worms	-	-	-	No equivalent recommended
Metoprolol	tab	100mg	HTN/AF/Angina/Migraine	-	-	-	No equivalent recommended
Metronidazole	tab	500mg	Infections	500*	200*	-	200mg tablets
Miconazole	crm	2%	Fungal skin infections	5*	2*	-	Vaginal cream 80g; pessaries also
Midazolam	amp	5mg/ml	Epileptic fits	20*	-	-	Diazepam 10mg/ml
Misoprostol	tab	200ug	Post-partum haemorrhage	-	-	-	No equivalent recommended
Morphine	amp	10mg/ml	Severe pain	20	10	-	
Morphine	liq	1mg/ml	Severe pain in patients able to eat and drink	-	-	-	
Naloxone	amp	0.4mg/ml	Opiate overdose	-	-	-	
Omeprazole	tab	20mg	Reflux, peptic ulcers	-	-	-	
Ondanestron	tab	4mg	Vomiting, sea-sickness	-	-	-	Cyclizine 50mg

Name	Form[a]	Strength	Indication[b]	second edition of the Guide[c]			Notes on the second edition of the Guide[d]
				A	B	C	
Oral Rehydration Solution	powder	sachet	Dehydration due to diarrhoea	50*	20*	5*	Each sachet makes 1litre
Oxymetazoline	nasal drop	0.50%	Nasal obstruction/drain sinuses	-	-	-	Only ephedrine tablets (A)
Paracetamol	tab	500mg	Pain and fever	300	150	100	
Permethrin	lot	1%	Lice	12*	2*	-	Lindane crm 60g tubes; also for scabies
Permethrin	lot	5%	Scabies	12*	2*	-	Lindane crm 60g tubes; also for lice
Povidone iodine	oint	10%	Disinfect skin/wounds	-	-	-	Iodine solution recommended
Povidone iodine	liq	10%	Disinfect skin/wounds	400ml*	200ml*	100ml*	Iodine solution
Prednisone	tab	25mg	Asthma/inflammatory conditions	-	-	-	Hydrocortisone injection only
Salbutamol	inh	100ug/dose	Asthma/bronchitis/ emphysema	2	1	-	
Sodium chloride	liq	0.9%, 1 Litre	Fluid replacement	6	2	-	
Tetracaine [amethocaine]	eye drop	0.50%	Eye examination	2	1	-	10ml bottles
Tetracycline	eye oint	1%	Minor eye infections	6	3	1	
Vitamin K	amp	10mg/ml	Reverse warfarin or similar	-	-	-	
Water for injection	amp	5ml	Reconstitute injections	30	20	-	
Zidovudine + lamivudine	tab	300mg/150mg	Needle-stick injury prophylaxis	-	-	-	No equivalent recommended
Zinc oxide	paste/oint	20%	Irritated skin	12	3	3	30g tubes of zinc oxide paste

a. amp=ampoule; crm=cream; drp=drop; ; inh=inhalation; liq=liquid; lct=lotion; oint=ointment; tab=tablet

b. AF=atrial fibrillation; HTN=hypertension; MI=myocardial infarction

c. Category of ship; see main text for definitions; quantities marked with an * indicate quantities based on alternative medicines mentioned in the notes section.

d. Letters in brackets (e.g. (A)) refer to the category of ship that the notes relate to; NSAID=non-steroidal antiinflammatory drug

Annex 2: Mapping of the medicines in the third edition of the Guide to the quantities recommended in the Australian and UK guidelines for ships

Name	Form[a]	Strength	Australian guidelines[b]			Note on the Australian guidelines[c]	UK guidelines[d]			Notes on the UK guidelines[e]
			A	B	C		A	B	C	
Acetylsalicylic acid	tab	300mg	-	-	-	Other NSAIDs recommended	-	-	-	Other NSAIDs recommended
Aciclovir	tab	400mg	-	-	-	No alternative recommended	-	-	-	No alternative recommended
Adrenaline	amp	1mg/ml	5+	5+	-		10+	5+	-	And/or Epipen® also carried
Amoxicillin/ clavulanic acid	tab	875mg/125mg	-	-	-	Alternative oral antibiotics recommended	-	-	-	Alternative oral antibiotics recommended
Artemether	amp	80mg/ml	-	-	-	No parenteral recommended	-	-	-	No parenteral recommended
Artemether + lumefantrine	tab	20mg/120mg	-	-	-	Alternative oral treatments recommended	-	-	-	Alternative oral treatments recommended
Atropine	amp	1.2mg/ml	15	15	-	Only for ships carrying dangerous goods	-	-	-	Only recommended for 'doctors bag'
Azithromycin	tab	500mg	100*	50*		Erythromycin 250mg tablets	28*	28*		Erythromycin 250mg tablets
Ceftriaxone	amp	1g	20	-	-	Cat. B carry benzyl penicillin	20*	-	-	Cefuroxime 750mg amp; Cat. B carry benzyl penicillin
Cetirizine	tab	10mg	30*+	30*+	-	Loratadine 10mg tablets	30+	30+	-	
Charcoal, activated	powder		200*	200*	-	300mg tablets; only for ships carrying dangerous goods	-	-	-	No alternative recommended
Ciprofloxacin	tab	250mg	28	14	-		20	10	-	
Cloves, oil of	liq		15ml	15ml+	-		10ml+	10ml+	-	
Dexamethasone	amp	4mg/ml	5*	-	-	Hydrocortisone 100mg amp	3*	1*	-	Hydrocortisone 100mg amp

Name	Form[a]	Strength	Australian guidelines[b]			Note on the Australian guidelines[c]	UK guidelines[d]			Notes on the UK guidelines[e]
			A	B	C		A	B	C	
Diazepam	tab	5mg	40+	20+	-	Also recommend 2x diazepam amp	23+	-	-	Also recommends 5x diazepam amp
Docusate with senna	tab	50mg/8mg	12*	-	-	Glycerine suppositories	12*	-	-	Glycerine suppositories
Doxycycline	tab	100mg	21	7	-		8	-	-	
Ethanol, hand cleanser	gel	70%	-	-	-	No equivalent recommended	-	-	-	No equivalent recommended
Ethanol	liq	70%	2400ml*+	1200ml*+	-	Cetrimide+chlorhexidine solution plus 100 alcohol impregnated swabs	100ml*	100ml*	-	Cetrimide+chlorhexidine solution or 100 impregnated swabs
Fluorescein	eye strip	1%	20*+	20*+	-	Individual disposable units	20	20	-	Individual disposable units
Frusemide	amp	40mg/4ml	5*	5*	-	20mg/2ml amps; also frusemide tabs	2*	-	-	20mg/2ml amps; also frusemide tabs
Glucagon	amp	1mg	-	-	-	No equivalent recommended	-	-	-	No equivalent recommended
Haloperidol	amp	5mg/ml	10*+	5*+	-	Chlorpromazine 25mg amps; also tabs	5*	-	-	Chlorpromazine 25mg amps; also tabs for Cat A and B
Hydrocortisone	crm	1%	2	1	-	30g tubes	2	-	-	30g tubes
Ibuprofen	tab	400mg	48	24	-	200mg or 400mg tabs; alternative NSAIDs also provided	100	50	50	Diclofenac suppositories also for Cat A
Isosorbide dinitrate	tab	5mg	2*	1*	1*	GTN sublingual spray	1*	1*	-	GTN spray or patches
Lignocaine	amp	1%, 5ml	25*	5*	-	2ml amps	5	5	-	Lignocaine gel for Cat A
Loperamide	tab	2mg	24	16	-	Also list codeine tabs	30	30	30	
Mebendazole	tab	100mg	6+	6+	-		6+	6+	-	
Metoprolol	tab	100mg	28*	-	-	Atenolol 50mg tabs	28*	-	-	Atenolol tablets

Name	Form[a]	Strength	Australian guidelines[b]			Note on the Australian guidelines[c]	UK guidelines[d]			Notes on the UK guidelines[e]
			A	B	C		A	B	C	
Metronidazole	tab	500mg	42*	21*	-	400mg tabs; tinidazole also recommended	21	21	-	Suppositories also for Cat A
Miconazole	crm	2%	2	1	-	30g tubes; vaginal preparations also recommended; benzoic acid oint also	2	1	-	30g tubes; Benzoic acid oint also
Midazolam	amp	5mg/ml	5*	5*	-	Diazepam 10mg rectal preparation	5*	5*	-	Diazepam 10mg rectal preparation
Misoprostol	tab	200mcg	-	-	-	No equivalent recommended	-	-	-	No equivalent recommended
Morphine	amp	10mg/ml	10	5	-		10	10		
Morphine	liq	1mg/ml	-	-	-	Codeine phosphate 30mg	-	-	-	Codeine phosphate 30mg
Naloxone	amp	0.4mg/ml	5	5	-		-	-	-	No equivalent recommended
Omeprazole	tab	20mg	-	-	-	Cimetidine 400mg	-	-	-	Cimetidine 400mg
Ondanestron	tab	4mg	-	-	-	Prochlorperazine 5mg	-	-	-	Prochlorperazine 3mg buccal tablets
Oral Rehydration Solution	powder	sachet	120	40	-	Each sachet makes 200ml	16-20	16-20	-	Each sachet makes 1L
Oxymetazoline	nasal drop	0.50%	2*+	1*+	-	Ephedrine 0.5% nasal drops	1*+	1*+	-	Ephedrine nasal drops
Paracetamol	tab	500mg	500	500	50		100	50	50	
Permethrin	lot	1%	200ml+	-	-		2+	-	-	2 bottle, size not stated
Permethrin	lot	5%	6*	2*	-	Permethrin 5% cream x 30g tubes	-	-	-	
Povidone iodine	oint	10%	-	-	-	Silver sulfadiazine cream for burns	-	-	-	Silver sulfadiazine cream for burns
Povidone iodine	liq	10%	2400ml*+	1200ml*+	-	Cetrimide+chlorhexidine solution; also used to disinfect	100ml*+	100ml*+	-	Cetrimide+chlorhexidine solution; also used to disinfect

Name	Form[a]	Strength	Australian guidelines[b]			Note on the Australian guidelines[c]	UK guidelines[d]			Notes on the UK guidelines[e]
			A	B	C		A	B	C	
Prednisone	tab	25mg	60*	60*	-	5mg tablets	28*	28*	-	5mg tablets
Salbutamol	inh	100mcg/dose	2	1	-		1	1	-	
Sodium chloride	liq	0.9%, 1 Litre	5*	3*	-	Only for ships carrying dangerous goods	-	-	-	
Tetracaine [amethocaine]	eye drop	0.50%	20+	20+	-	Unit dose minims	20	20		Unit dose minims
Tetracycline	eye oint	1%	5*	2*	-	Framycetin eye ointment	4*	1*	-	Chloramphenicol eye ointment
Vitamin K	amp	10mg/ml	10*	-	-	Only paediatric recommended; adult strength only for carrying dangerous goods	-	-	-	Only paediatric recommended
Water for injection	amp	5ml	20	5	-	For reconstituting benzyl penicillin	-	-	-	
Zidovudine + lamivudine	tab	300mg/150mg	-	-	-	No equivalent recommended	-	-	-	No equivalent recommended
Zinc oxide	paste/ oint	20%	100g+	100g+	-		25g+	-	-	

a. amp=ampoule; crm=cream; drp=drop; inh=inhalation; liq=liquid; lot=lotion; oint=ointment; strp=strip; tab=tablet

b. Quantities are based on 20 crew for Category A unless otherwise marked; quantities marked with a '+' are recommended irrespective of crew size; quantities marked with '*' are those for an alternative drug/dose/indication described in the Notes section; GTN=glyceryl trinitrate

c. NSAID=non-steroidal anti-inflammatory drug

d. Quantities are per 10 crew for Category A and B ships unless otherwise marked; Quantities marked with a '+' are recommended irrespective of crew size; quantities marked with '*' are those for an alternative drug/dose/indication described in the Notes section; GTN=glyceryl trinitrate

Annex 3: Recommended quantities of medicines for the third edition of the *International Medical Guide for Ships*

Name	Form[a]	Strength	Indication[b]	Quantities per 10 crew[c]			Notes
				A	B	C	
Acetylsalicylic acid	tab	300mg	Pain, fever, blood clots	50	50	-	
Aciclovir	tab	400mg	Herpes simplex/zoster	70+	35+	-	
Adrenaline	amp	1mg/ml	Anaphylaxis	10+	5+	5+	
Amoxicillin/clavulanic acid	tab	875mg/125mg	Infections	20	10	-	
Artemether	amp	80mg/ml	Malaria treatment	12+	12+	-	
Artemether + lumefantrine	tab	20mg/120mg	Malaria treatment	24+	24+	-	Double if crew size >30
Atropine	amp	1.2mg/ml	MI/organophosphate poisoning	10+	5+	-	Double quantity if carrying organophosphates
Azithromycin	tab	500mg	Infections	10+	5+	-	Double if crew size >30
Ceftriaxone	amp	1g	Infections	15	5+	-	
Cetirizine	tab	10mg	Hayfever/hives/dermatitis	30+	30+	-	
Charcoal, activated	powder		Poisoning	120g+	120g+	-	
Ciprofloxacin	tab	250mg	Infections	20+	10+	-	Double if crew size >30
Cloves, oil of	liq		Toothache	10ml	10ml+	-	
Dexamethasone	amp	4mg/ml	Severe asthma/anaphylaxis	3	1	-	
Diazepam	tab	5mg	Alcohol withdrawal	50+	20+	-	
Docusate with senna	tab	50mg/8mg	Constipation	30+	-	-	
Doxycycline	tab	100mg	Infections	10	-	-	
Ethanol, hand cleanser	gel	70%	Hand cleaning	500ml	500ml+	100ml+	
Ethanol	liq	70%	Disinfect instruments	500ml	100ml	-	
Fluorescein	eye strips	1%	Detect corneal damage	20+	20+	-	

Name	Form[a]	Strength	Indication[b]	Quantities per 10 crew[c]			Notes
				A	B	C	
Frusemide	amp	40mg/4ml	Pulmonary oedema	5+	5+	-	
Glucagon	amp	1mg	Hypoglycaemia	1+	1+	-	
Haloperidol	amp	5mg/ml	Psychosis/severe agitation	5	5+	-	
Hydrocortisone	crm	1%	Allergy/inflammatory skin	2 x 30g	1 x 30g	-	One tube per patient
Ibuprofen	tab	400mg	Inflammation/pain	100	50	50+	
Isosorbide dinitrate	tab	5mg	Angina/MI	10	10	5+	
Lignocaine	amp	1%, 5ml	Suturing/minor surgery	5	5	-	
Loperamide	tab	2mg	Diarrhoea	30	30	10+	
Mebendazole	tab	100mg	Intestinal worms	6+	6+	-	
Metoprolol	tab	100mg	HTN/AF/Angina/Migraine	60+	-	-	
Metronidazole	tab	500mg	Infections	30+	20+	-	
Miconazole	crm	2%	Fungal skin infections	2 x 30g	1 x 30g	-	Double quantities if females on board
Midazolam	amp	5mg/ml	Epileptic fits	10+	5+	-	
Misoprostol	tab	200ug	Post-partum haemorrhage	3+	3+	-	Only if females on board
Oral Rehydration Solution	powder	sachet	Dehydration due to diarrhoea	15l (75)	10l (50)	2l (10)+	Quantities in brackets are number of sachets based on sachets made up to 200ml
Oxymetazoline	nasal drop	0.50%	Nasal obstruction/drain sinuses	2	1	-	One bottle per patient
Morphine	amp	10mg/ml	Severe pain	10	10	-	
Morphine	liq	1mg/ml	Severe pain in patients able to eat and drink	100ml+	100ml+	-	
Naloxone	amp	0.4mg/ml	Opiate overdose	10+	5+	-	
Omeprazole	tab	20mg	Reflux, peptic ulcers	30+	30+	-	

Name	Form[a]	Strength	Indication[b]	Quantities per 10 crew[c]			Notes
				A	B	C	
Ondanestron	tab	4mg	Vomiting, sea-sickness	10	10	10+	
Paracetamol	tab	500mg	Pain and fever	100	50	25	
Permethrin	lot	1%	Lice	200ml+	100ml+	-	Double if crew size >30
Permethrin	lot	5%	Scabies	300ml+	100ml+	-	100ml per patient
Povidone iodine	oint	10%	Disinfect skin/wounds	1 x 25g	1x25g	-	
Povidone iodine	liq	10%	Disinfect skin/wounds	100ml	100ml	100ml+	
Prednisone	tab	25mg	Asthma/inflammatory conditions	30+	30+	-	
Salbutamol	inh	100ug/dose	Asthma/bronchitis/ emphysema	1	1	-	One inhaler per patient
Sodium chloride	liq	0.9%, 1 litre	Fluid replacement	5+	1	-	
Tetracaine [amethocaine]	eye drop	0.50%	Eye examination	20+	20+	-	
Tetracycline	eye oint	1%	Minor eye infections	2	1	1+	One tube per patient
Vitamin K	amp	10mg/ml	Reverse warfarin or similar	2+	2+	-	
Water for injection	amp	5ml	Reconstitute injections	10	5+	-	Only used to reconstitute ceftriaxone
Zidovudine + lamivudine	tab	300mg/150mg	Needle-stick injury prophylaxis	56+	56+	-	
Zinc oxide	paste/oint	20%	Irritated skin	200g+	100g+	100g+	4 x 25g or 3 x 30g tubes per 100g

a. amp=ampoule; crm=cream; inh=inhalation; liq=liquid; lot=lotion; oint=ointment; tab=tablet

b. AF=atrial fibrillation; HTN=hypertension; MI=myocardial infarction

c. Category of ship; see main text for definitions; quantities marked with an '+' are suggested quantities irrespective of crew size. The assumed duration of each trip is up to 3-4 weeks.

References

1. McKay MP. Maritime Health Emergencies. *Occupational Medicine*. 2007;57(6):453.
2. Hall TM, Herring SA, Jozwiak TJ. Basic Elements of Maritime Health Care. *Journal of Occupational and Environmental Medicine*. 1984;26(3):202.
3. Scott J, Lucas R, Snoots R. Maritime Medicine. *Emergency medicine clinics of North America*. 1997;15(1):241-9.
4. Lateef F, Anantharaman V. Maritime Radio-Medical Services: The Singapore General Hospital Experience. *American Journal of Emergency Medicine*. 2002;20(4):349-51.
5. Guidance Notes on Medical Facilities Aboard Ships. February 2002. Australian Maritime Safety Authority. (http://www.comlaw.gov.au/Comlaw/Legislation/LegislativeInstrument1.nsf/0/279E72D189C84BBBCA257161007DDC39/$file/Mo10+13of+01.pdf, accessed 01 December 2009)
6. Merchant Shipping Notice 1768 (M+F) : Ships' Medical Stores. August 2003. Maritime and Coastguard Agency. (http://www.mcga.gov.uk/c4mca/1768.pdf, accessed 01 December 2009)
7. The Ship's Medicine Chest and Medical Aid at Sea. 2003. U.S. Department of Health and Human Services. (http://www.operationalmedicine.org/Library/VNH%20Textbooks/Ships_Medicine_Chest_2003edition.pdf, accessed 01 December 2009)
8. Maritime Pharmacy: Towards Cooperation and Standardization Globally. 2003. Working Group Ships Medicines - International Pharmaceutical Federation (http://geneesmiddel-en.wewi.eldoc.ub.rug.nl/FILES/root/Rapporten/2002/scheepskist/Finalreport9320.doc, accessed 20 December 2009)
9. Guidance to the International Medical Guides for Ships third Edition: Interim Advice on the Best Use of the Medical Chest for Ocean-Going Merchant Vessels without a Doctor Onboard. WHO Collaborating Centre for the Health of Seafarers and the International Maritime Health Association. (http://imha.net/images/stories/Guidance%20re%20IMGS%20Medical%20Chest.pdf, accessed 20 December 2009)
10. Artemether for severe malaria. (http://www.medicine.ox.ac.uk/bandolier/booth/alternat/At127.html, accessed 20 December 2009)
11. Artemether 80mg/ml injection/1ml/Box-8. (http://www.supply.unicef.dk/catalogue/item.asp?c1=2&c2=6&c3=70&catno=1300069&head=Artemether+80mg%2Fml+injection%2F1ml%2FBOX-8, accessed 01 December 2009)
12. MGN257(M): Prevention of Infectious Disease at Sea by Immunisations and Anti-Malaria Medication (Prophylaxis). Maritime and Coastguard Agency (http://www.mcga.gov.uk/c4mca/mgn257.pdf, accessed 20 December 2009)